On Foreign Soil

On Foreign Soil:

AMERICAN GARDENERS ABROAD

May Brawley Hill

HARRY N. ABRAMS, INC., PUBLISHERS

For B

*T*o see another's garden may give
us a keen perception of the richness
or poverty of his personality, of his
experiences and associations in life,
and of his spiritual qualities.

Charles Downing Lay,
A Garden Book (1924)

Frontispiece: ALEXIS NICOLAS PERIGNON THE ELDER.
The Potager of the Château de Valentinois, Passy, c. 1780.
Gouache on paper. National Gallery of Art, Washington, D.C.

Page 6: The walled garden at Floors Castle, Kelso, Scotland.
Country Life Picture Library, London

May Goelet married the eighth duke of Roxburgh in
1903 and undertook the remodeling of the grounds at
Floors Castle, which included this garden noted for its
perennial borders.

Editor: Barbara Burn
Designer: Christine Knorr
Production Manager: Maria Pia Gramaglia

Library of Congress Cataloging-in-Publication Data

Hill, May Brawley.
  On foreign soil : American gardens abroad / May Brawley Hill.
    p. cm.
  Includes bibliographical references and index.
  ISBN 0-8109-5898-8 (hardcover : alk. paper)
  1. Gardens, American–Europe. 2. Landscape
gardening–Europe. I. Title.

SB457.53.H552 2005
712'.0973'094–dc22

2004026018

Text copyright © 2005 by May Brawley Hill

Printed and bound in China
10 9 8 7 6 5 4 3 2 1

Harry N. Abrams, Inc.
100 Fifth Avenue
New York, N.Y. 10011
www.abramsbooks.com

Abrams is a subsidiary of

CONTENTS

INTRODUCTION

*F*ifteen years ago, while visiting a friend in La Malbaie, Quebec, I was taken to see a garden made by an American, Frank Cabot. I spent the long summer afternoon wandering through the garden in an ecstasy of discovery and delight. Although I had been trained as an art historian, I had never before been so deeply moved by a work of art, certainly not by one conceived on so grand a scale. Within a sequence of immensely satisfying, articulated spaces that encouraged exploration, the subtlety of the plantings and the range of their forms, colors, and brilliant combinations repeatedly brought me to a halt for a closer look. My visit became a passionate quest, punctuated by visual, tactile, aural, and mental experiences that evoked strong emotions. From every viewpoint, I saw constantly changing pictures of remarkable beauty, heightened by a symphony of scents and the counterpoint of water—still or tumbling, gushing or dripping, or just flowing quietly.

The experience changed the course of my life, for I have spent the intervening years in an attempt to understand the power of that garden. This process of self-education has so far led me to write several articles and two books on American gardens. The topic of this volume was inspired by Frank's garden and also by that of my cousin Sheppard Craige, who has made a similar commitment to gardening abroad, in the Tuscan hill town of San Giovanni d'Asso. Their examples aroused my curiosity about gardens made by other Americans living abroad and spurred me to travel to a number of very different gardens.

The very act of making a personal garden implies that the maker feels at home. It seems to me that to make a garden in a foreign country, where climate, plants, and soil—to say nothing of culture and language—are unfamiliar requires a particular set of circumstances as well as a special character. This book is the result of my investigation into the varied circumstances of certain Americans abroad—fascinating characters who have made gardens in England, France, and Italy since the earliest days of our nation. I limited the scope to those three countries, as they were the principal ones visited in the early years of American independence, and because they are still easily accessible for American travelers. The gardeners, selected from an over-whelming number of possible choices, were those who were directly involved in the creation of their gardens. As a result, the gardens, like autobiographies, reveal the personalities, values, experiences, and often spiritual qualities of their creators.

America's relationship to the culture of Europe has been an ambivalent one from the early days of settlement. The North American continent offered boundless space, untrammeled nature, and limitless potential to European colonists. Although they established a society that was more open and less class bound than the ones they had left behind, the colonists neverthe-less sought to re-create in the New World the civilized comforts of the Old. In pleasure gar-dening, as in the other fine arts, America followed the lead of Europe. Our fine arts have been distinctly American since Independence, but only in the last century have we as a nation man-aged to overcome our sense of inferiority in art and architecture. In gardening, although we are now aware of vibrant indigenous styles and can boast preeminent contemporary designers, we still look to Europe and especially England for inspiration. But from the beginning, traffic and influence have flowed in both directions.

In 1640 Captain George Evelyn, who grew up in America, where his father had settled in 1610, returned to England to visit his cousins George and John Evelyn at Wotton in Surrey. Here he joined in the remaking of their garden and designed a portico for a grotto with Doric columns and a frieze, the first use in England of a Doric temple façade as a garden feature. The interior of the grotto was decorated with a fresco of Venus riding a dolphin, a scene shocking to the Puritan sensibilities of John Evelyn, who recorded his disapproval in his diary. Captain George had benefited from travel in Italy, among the first of many garden makers, both English and American, who would learn from the classical remains and the gardens there.[1]

Americans since the earliest days have traveled abroad to experience at first hand the cul-tural riches and architectural treasures of Europe, and a surprising number have elected to stay on for many years, even a lifetime. Before 1900 Europe offered career opportunities that were nonexistent in America, particularly in literature and the arts. It provided as well a boun-ty of sensual and aesthetic experiences unavailable at home. For some Americans, the social contacts they made in Europe enhanced their status on their return. For many, it was only in Europe that they could re-invent themselves, unconstrained by class, gender, or social norms prevailing in America. A stay in Europe was particularly liberating for women, both for those who pioneered in the arts and for many single women who enjoyed access to cultural resources and a freedom of movement not yet countenanced in America. At the end of the nineteenth century, as pressures of industrialization and economic competition intensified, many Americans with keen aesthetic sensibilities and little tolerance for modern hustle and noise retreated to Europe. Displaced patricians with independent incomes sought a refuge where their class was not yet threatened by vulgar plutocrats or masses of immigrants. And, of course, artists continued to find kindred spirits and congenial surroundings abroad. Even today the siren call of sensual experience continues to draw Americans to the cultural feasts of Europe, and the lures of romance and marriage, or of a career, remain compelling reasons for staying abroad.

Gardens made by these expatriates over several centuries in three different countries demonstrate their American origins, not through any identifiable style but rather in the way the gardens were made. Our democratic tendencies tend to make us tolerant and adaptable; most Americans make an effort to fit into the local milieu when living abroad. But Americans value individuality and, lacking a long history of pleasure gardening, blithely mix local usages with quirky innovations and eclectic borrowings from other traditions. On the whole, Americans are a risk-taking lot: it was risky to settle in the New World, but it is also risky to leave one's home and country to make a life abroad. In their gardens, Americans abroad often push the limits, trying all sorts of plants, combining disparate styles, going all out in following a particular passion. A hands-on approach is characteristic; often expatriates jump in and work alongside their gardeners, or even do the gardening themselves. Americans are not noted for their patience. When they want results, they want them yesterday. In their gardens abroad, they seldom hesitate to plant full-grown trees or to fill every space with their favorites, regardless of local custom or horticultural dictate.

These American gardens abroad are as various as their makers' circumstances and motives for living in Europe. Some of the expatriates who went abroad to establish careers made gardens both as a sign of success and as an adjunct to a genteel life. Others used their gardens to show off their aesthetic and cultural sophistication or to display their wealth. The most appealing expatriate gardens are those grown out of personal necessity; some of these were made by artists who could not resist painting a picture or shaping the space of their surroundings. Others were private worlds that offered their makers an escape from the unpleasant realities of the industrial present. For all, the making of a garden provided a refuge for the spirit. As Frank Cabot perceptively remarked about his own garden at La Malbaie, "to be there is to come home."[2] ⊘

WILLIAM HANNAN. *North Front of West Wycombe House Viewed Across the Lake with a Wooden Bridge and the Rotondo* (detail, see page 23)

THE FIRST AMERICANS ABROAD

Chapter One

"What then is the American, this new man?
He is either an European, or the descendant of an European....
Here individuals of all nations are melted into a new race of men."

St. Jean de Crèvecoeur, *Letters From an American Farmer* (1782)

ENGLAND, THE HOME COUNTRY

The "howling wilderness" faced by the earliest settlers in America presented a formidable challenge to making a home. Clearing land and growing crops demanded an intimate accommodation to the very foreign soil and climate, and separate pleasure gardens were slow to appear. By the early 1700s, however, colonial governors such as Alexander Spottswood in Williamsburg, Virginia, and planters such as Henry Middleton at Middleton Place in South Carolina could command terraced gardens with canals, fish ponds, arbors, summerhouses, and decorative sculpture modeled on those of the English landed gentry. Settlers of the original thirteen colonies hailed from Holland, Germany, and France, and elsewhere in Europe, as well as Great Britain, but culturally England remained the home country. Her literature, fine arts, fashions, furnishings, and gardens provided the standards by which educated and affluent colonists judged their own.

By the mid-1700s, the growing European demand for the horticultural riches of the new world made Boston, New York, Philadelphia, Charleston, and Savannah centers for the exchange of seeds, plants, and botanical knowledge. Among the first American plants sent to Europe were corn, beans, squash, tobacco, and other natives useful for food or medicine. Forest giants, including tulip poplar, white oak, and many evergreens quickly followed. The forest understory provided a cornucopia of ornamental trees and flowering shrubs, while

COPLESTONE WARRE BAMPFYLDE.
*View of the Garden at Stourhead with
the Temple of Apollo, the Palladian
Bridge, and the Pantheon,* 1775.
Watercolor on paper. National Trust
Photo Library, Angelo Hornak

meadows, woods, and wetlands furnished a wealth of spring- and fall-blooming perennials to enrich the English pleasure garden. John Bartram of Philadelphia, the most important plantsman of the day, supplied seeds for the fashionable "American" gardens being made by British horticultural enthusiasts on many estates at mid-century. He and other noted nurserymen were kept busy at home furnishing plants and seeds to the country estates and elegant town gardens that proliferated in the colonies. A typical lot in town would be fenced and a pleasure garden of parterre beds placed at the side or in front of the house. Rural mansions were usually built on prominences with terraces, or "falls" as they were called in the south, on the garden front. Entrance drives were lined with trees, and axial paths were bordered with clipped evergreens.

By the mid-1700s in England, however, a landscape revolution was taking place that would eventually affect a few affluent and well-traveled colonial gardeners.[1] Influential British writers such as Joseph Addison, in a reaction against the formal geometries of the old style, began to advocate the visual incorporation of fields and woodlands into the gardens surrounding the country house. Grounds were laid out by eye, as a painter would compose a picture, rather than with level and line. In the 1740s, English landowners, working with designers such as William Kent, visually joined their gardens with outlying fields and distant prospects to create a series of views suggestive of landscapes by the French painters Claude Lorrain or Nicolas Poussin. By the 1760s, the influence of Lancelot "Capability" Brown, who improved scores of estates with undulating hills, serpentine streams, and irregular groves of trees, could be seen throughout England.

While Thomas Jefferson was planning the site for Monticello in 1767, he encountered this more naturalistic style in the writings of William Shenstone, who had adapted the new ideas to his small property, The Leasowes, in Warwickshire.[2] Here Shenstone had created a *ferme ornée*, or ornamental farm, where the open fields were visually incorporated into the garden through the use of sunken fences, or ha-has. Attractive groupings of trees were planted, and paths meandered through the woods and fields, dotted with decorative structures and seats from which the stroller could admire the picturesque effects. Jefferson was already well aware of the use of decorative ruins, temples, and grottos to arouse emotions and to recall historical associations in these landscaped English estates, and he planned several for Monticello, including a Gothic outbuilding to be surrounded by "gloomy evergreens."[3]

Although Jefferson did not travel to England until after the American Revolution, other American landowners who could afford the time and expense of a visit toured these newly designed gardens and adapted elements of the new style to their own homes. Richard Stockton of

BENJAMIN WEST. *Mr. West's Garden, Gallery and Painting Room*, c. 1795. Oil on canvas. National Portrait Gallery, Smithsonian Institution, Washington, D.C.

West added three exhibition rooms and a studio, connected with an arcaded passageway to the house, enclosing his garden on three sides. West's family and students are shown at leisure enjoying the flower borders and oval lawn.

Princeton, New Jersey, made improvements at his estate, Morven, following a visit to Alexander Pope's garden at Twickenham. Henry Lucas of Charleston, South Carolina, visited both Lord Burlington's famous garden at Chiswick and The Leasowes before he began his own garden at Mepkin on the Cooper River.[+]

Many American travelers to England before the Revolution, however, were not wealthy landowners who had estates awaiting their return, but young men beginning their careers in trade or in the arts. For American-born painters and writers, such a move was a necessity, as recognition came only with European study and contacts. Once established in England, many enjoyed the pleasures of a town or country garden as a sign of their financial success and their arduously acquired status as gentlemen.

BENJAMIN WEST. *Mr. West's Family in the Garden of Their Residence in Newman Street*, c. 1785–88.
Pen and wash on paper. The Toledo Museum of Art, Toledo, Ohio, gift of Edward Drummond Libbey

West is seen on the right under an umbrella; his wife and two sons stand by the entrance of the exhibition rooms accompanied by numerous pets.

Painter Benjamin West found small scope for his talent in his native Philadelphia, where little distinction was made between sign painting and fine art. West was an unknown quantity when he arrived in London in 1763 after three years of study in Italy, but the austere Neoclassical style he had learned there caught the eye of King George III. Less than ten years after his arrival, West was appointed Painter of History to the King, and he later achieved the prestigious post of president of the Royal Academy of Art.

West's commodious house at 14 Newman Street lodged a succession of American students who came abroad for study. West and his pupils worked in two lofty painting rooms that he had added to the north side of the house. The windows overlooked an arcade and a garden featuring the classical sculpture and urns that West had acquired in Italy, evidence of the importance

JOHN GREENWOOD. *The Seven Sisters of Tottenham*, c. 1790.
Oil on canvas. Museum of New Zealand Te Papa Tongarewa, Wellington, New Zealand

The seven sisters were the elms in a circle on the left. Greenwood shows himself on horseback, his wife and daughters looking at the swans, and his son and nurse in the doorway of his country house. Its front garden is enclosed by a picket fence.

of the classical past to his art. The garden's central feature was a manicured lawn bordered with flowering shrubs and plants in pots. A visitor in the 1790s described the garden as "very small but elegant, with a grass-plot in the middle, and busts upon stands under an arcade."[5]

West's garden was a model of order and decorum, as was his life. The same cannot be said of his most successful pupil, Gilbert Stuart of Newport, Rhode Island, who had boarded with West for five years until 1782. Stuart's informal and brilliantly painted *Portrait of a Gentleman Skating*, exhibited at the Royal Academy that year, brought him immediate renown and a demand for his portraits. Stuart's increasing income allowed him to maintain a grand house on New Burlington Street and supported his riotous lifestyle until 1787, when he was obliged to flee to Ireland to escape his creditors. The Irish artist J. D. Herbert visited Stuart on his farm near Dublin and found him tending his flowers, a bucolic respite from a hectic life. Herbert related that Stuart's garden was "well-cropped, all by his own hands." When Herbert confessed that he would rather see Stuart's paintings than his grounds, Stuart replied that "[he] pitied me very much, observing what a loss I sustained by not attending to the cultivation of that on which mankind were supported."[6] Like other Americans abroad living in difficult circumstances, Stuart found solace in his garden, which he cultivated himself. Even if cash had not been in short supply, he would probably have done the same, as he seemed to love the work.

John Greenwood, a painter from Boston who, like West, arrived in London in 1763, achieved success as an art dealer and auctioneer with two London sales rooms and a thriving business in European paintings. Until his marriage in 1769, Greenwood had intended to return to America, where his mother still lived. Although he consorted with fellow Americans at the New England Coffee House in London, he nevertheless felt a deep attachment to his country home and garden.[7] His last painting, *The Seven Sisters of Tottenham* of 1790, presents a bucolic view of a circle of seven ancient elms, a noted landmark opposite his house on Page Green. The front garden of his house, full of hollyhocks and other summer blooms, was enclosed with a picket fence. In a scene of domestic tranquility, Greenwood included himself on a horse, as his son is led into the house by the nurse and his wife and daughters look out over the pond.[8]

John Singleton Copley, whose aspirations reached higher than becoming the most accomplished portrait painter in the colonies, moved to London in 1775 with his loyalist father-in-law, his wife, and two children. Copley congratulated himself in a letter to his half-brother, exclaiming, "Could anything be more fortunate than the time of my leaving Boston? Poor America!"[9] Nonetheless, he remained attached to the country he had abandoned. On December 5, 1782,

after hearing King George III acknowledge America's independence in the House of Lords, he rushed to his studio and added an American flag to the mast of a ship in the background of a portrait of his friend Elkanah Watson.[10]

Elkanah Watson was a young entrepreneur from Massachusetts who had gone to France in 1779 carrying dispatches from the Continental Congress to Benjamin Franklin, the American commissioner in Paris. Watson intended to make his fortune in France and established a mercantile business in the thriving port of Nantes, procuring supplies for the Continental Army, as well as French goods for sale in America. Entrusted with official dispatches from Franklin to the peace commissioners in London in 1782, Watson noted in his journal on arriving in England, "This was the land of our rancorous foe…; still, it is the land of our forefathers."[11]

Many American visitors and residents at the close of the century shared this deep ambivalence toward England, none more so than John Adams, who was appointed Ambassador to the Court of Saint James in 1785 following a seven-year stint in Paris. He wrote to Jefferson after two years of frustrating negotiations with the British government over trade: "There are four or five persons here with whom I hold a friendly intercourse and shall leave with some degree of pain, but I am not at home in this country." His wife, Abigail, put it in homelier terms: "Retiring to our little farm, feeding my poultry, and improving my garden has more charms for my fancy than residing at the Court of Saint James, where I seldom meet with characters as inoffensive as my hens and chickens, or minds so well improved as my garden."[12] (The Adamses had, however, enjoyed their earlier stay at Auteuil, near Paris and the Bois de Boulogne, where the house had a lovely, if overgrown, five-acre garden with fountains, flower beds, grape arbors, and a fish pond.)

Wealthy Americans who lived for a time in England after the Revolution tended to focus on the aspects of English life of which they could approve and emulate on their return home, especially country estates and their improved parkland. William Bingham, who had made a huge fortune during the Revolution, arrived in London in 1783 from Philadelphia with his beautiful nineteen-year-old wife, Anne Willing. They managed to be presented to King George III and, on a trip to Paris, to Louis XVI, which set a heady precedent for newly wealthy Americans eager for social certification. Before settling in Cavendish Square, the Binghams made a tour of nearby country estates in the company of John Penn, grandson of the founder of Pennsylvania. The following spring they made another tour, storing up images for their return to America.[13]

On their return to Philadelphia in 1786, the Binghams moved into their newly built and aptly named Mansion House with its three acres of gardens. Visitors noted an estate "in the best English style," its gardens "rich with curious and rare clumps of trees" and allées of imported Lombardy poplars.[14] John Penn, who had come back to Philadelphia the previous year, built a house and laid out the grounds of his estate, Solitude, in the latest style, with groves of trees and curving paths.[15]

Americans in temporary residence through necessity sought the society of their fellow expatriates. Benjamin West and John Singleton Copley were always very helpful in arranging introductions. One of the noted American hostesses was Angelica Schuyler Church, whose father had served with distinction as a major general during the Revolution. She had eloped at eighteen with Englishman John Barker Church and, when hostilities ended, went with him to London, where he subsequently became a Member of Parliament.[16] Another hospitable refuge was the home in Cavendish Square of John Paradise, a Greek-born Englishman who had become a naturalized American citizen, and his wife, Lucy Ludwell, who had inherited her father's estate, Green Spring, near Williamsburg.[17] On Sunday evenings John and Lucy Paradise offered a supper *à la Virginienne* to a lively mix of scientists, artists, writers, and diplomats. At gatherings like these, Americans could keep abreast of the latest political and cultural events and make useful social contacts. Thomas Jefferson, on his brief and unsuccessful trade mission to London from Paris in the spring of 1786, was a frequent guest.

When Jefferson was presented to George III at an official reception, the monarch could not have been "more ungracious."[18] Following the king's lead, few Englishmen of rank or official position would speak with Jefferson, or Adams either, if they could help it. Jefferson turned the trip to good account by traveling with Adams to most of the landscape gardens described in Thomas Whately's *Observations on Modern Gardening* (1770). Jefferson had purchased this important formulation of the aims and methods of the new style soon after it was published and used it as a guidebook.

Having visited nearly two dozen estates, Jefferson wrote in May 1786 that English gardening "is the article in which it excels all the earth. I mean their pleasure gardening. This, indeed, went far beyond my ideas."[19] John Adams was less impressed. At Stowe he commented that the temples to Venus and Bacchus were hardly necessary, as mankind had "no need of artificial incitements to such amusements." Although he found The Leasowes most appealing, he confided to his diary, "It will be long, I hope, before Ridings, Parks, Pleasure Grounds, Gardens, and ornamented Farms grow so much in fashion in America."[20]

The Napoleonic conflicts and the War of 1812 disrupted trade and discouraged American travel abroad. Nonetheless, many American artists and writers in the early 1800s still found it necessary to study and work for a time in England. Painter Washington Alston spent eleven years there, returning to Boston in 1818. His friend Washington Irving went in 1815 to London, which was the publishing capital of the English-speaking world, and was among the first in a succession of American writers whose acclaim in England assured later success in America. Between visits to his publishers and socializing among the resident American families, Irving toured picturesque locales in Wales and Scotland, as well as landscape gardens. After visiting The Leasowes, he noted the walks and "scenic effects" in his journal. In the book that was the first result of his stay in England, *The Sketchbook of Geoffrey Crayon* (1819–20), Irving reiterated the general view that the "taste of the English in what is called landscape gardening, is unrivalled." This he described as "the cherishing and training of some trees; . . . the nice distribution of flowers and plants of tender and graceful foliage; the introduction of a green slope of velvet turf; the partial opening of a peep of blue distance, or silver gleam of water."[21] All of these elements could be found in the picturesque landscape he created around his rural retreat, Sunnyside, in Tarrytown, New York, after his return to America.

As the capital of world trade, London was a financial as well as literary and artistic magnet for ambitious Americans. Joshua Bates and George Peabody were two of the American merchant bankers who established themelves there in the 1830s. Bates had arrived in 1816 and by 1828 was a full partner in Baring Brothers, acting for the United States government in England. Bates's country house at East Sheen, a London suburb, had landscaped grounds that included, in 1848, arabesque flower-beds near the house.[22] By this date flower beds were making a comeback and often burst from the confined geometry of circles or squares into patterns reminiscent of paisley shawls.

Peabody, a dry-goods merchant from Baltimore, had gone to England in 1837 and established offices in the City of London that became a center for visiting Americans. In 1854 he took as partner young Junius Spencer Morgan from Boston. Their firm specialized in American stocks and bonds, and steadfastly bought them at steep discounts through the Panic of 1857. The partners found themselves exceedingly wealthy as the American economy began to recover. Peabody, a bachelor, did not alter his living arrangement, but Morgan bought a mansion at Prince's Gate overlooking Hyde Park and a grand Georgian residence and estate, Dover House, near Roehampton.[23]

The south front of Dover House. From *Gardeners' Chronicle*, April 2, 1910. Royal Horticultural Society, Lindley Library, London

An araucaria draped in vines centers the formal garden dating from the 1860s. The beds would have been replanted several times a year with bulbs and annuals in decorative patterns.

Shortly after Morgan's death, an article in the *Gardeners' Chronicle* describing his 170-acre property illustrated another revolution in British gardening. The influx of tender plants and exotic trees from southern latitudes had spurred John Claudius Loudon, among other writers and landscape professionals, to develop the "gardenesque" style, an outgrowth of the picturesque layout, to display exotics to advantage as individual specimens. Greenhouse-raised annuals in blazing colors were set out in carpet beds or ribbon borders to create a carefully orchestrated display that remained unchanged for weeks. The pleasure gardens at Dover House had retained the flower garden on the south front of the house designed in 1863 for the display of spring bulbs followed by "carpet bedding which was well done and looked very pretty."[24] Its central bed held a monkey-puzzle (araucaria) tree, a specimen of great popularity at mid-century, which by 1910 was decrepit and draped with vines. ◌

FRANCE, THE REVOLUTIONARY PRESENT

As the leading citizens of the fledgling United States embarked on the creation of a new republic free from the rigid class distinctions of monarchy, they sought as well to encourage the development of a distinctive American culture. In a letter written to a friend in 1785, Thomas Jefferson advised against sending a young man to Europe. "He acquires a fondness for

Pleasure grounds of Dover House. From *Gardeners' Chronicle*, April 2, 1910. Royal Horticultural Society, Lindley Library, London

This part of the garden was developed later with beds for flowering shrubs and variegated plants. Specimen trees are newly planted. The path leads from the house to the rose garden, orchard, walled *potager*, and other areas of the eighteen-acre pleasure grounds.

European luxury and dissipation, and a contempt for the simplicity of his own country. He is fascinated with the privileges of the European aristocrats, and sees with abhorrence, the lovely equality which the poor enjoy with the rich in his own country."[25] Two years later, the lawyer and playwright Royall Tyler, an unsuccessful suitor for the hand of John and Abigail Adams's daughter, asked in his play *The Contrast*, "Why should our thoughts to distant countries roam / When each refinement may be found at home?"[26]

Revolutionary fervor encouraged such sentiments, but France, as an ally, attracted Americans in droves and offered a banquet of cultural refinements, both high and low, that were not available at home. Elkanah Watson believed that residence in France could do much to improve the American character. He wrote that familiarity with French culture would "enable us, as a nation, to shake off the leading-strings of Britain—the English sternness and formality of manner, retaining however sufficient of their gravity, to produce, with French ease and elegance, a happy compound of national character and manners."[27]

All visitors to Paris counted among the city's greatest amenities its magnificent public gardens. As an American resident in 1836 asked, "Who would live in this rank old Paris if it were not for its gardens?"[28] These included the fifty-acre Tuileries gardens bordering the Seine, designed by André Le Nôtre; the tree-lined Champs-Elysées leading to the seventeen-hundred-

BENJAMIN FRANKLIN. *Garden at Passy*. Inscribed "Benjamin Franklin fecit 27 March 1782." Pencil on paper. American Philosophical Society, Philadelphia

acre Bois de Boulogne; and the gardens of the Palais-Royal. These gardens served as settings for entertainment and socializing, none more so than that of the Palais-Royal, where the ground floors of the buildings that enclosed the garden housed shops, the second floors restaurants, and the third elegant bordellos. The gardens of the Palais de Luxembourg, a royal residence until the French Revolution, would later join the Palais-Royal as a place of rendezvous.[29]

Outside the city, Le Nôtre's formal gardens at Versailles were the most visited. American painter John Vanderlyn was struck by their "beauty and grandeur" and exclaimed in a letter to his brother, "The imagination cannot conceive anything so enchanting."[30] During his first stay in Paris, Elkanah Watson toured the gardens at Marly and St. Cloud, where he was most impressed by the water features—cascades, fountains, and *jets d'eau.*[31]

It was in private estates in and around Paris, however, that one could find English-style picturesque gardens. There was at this time a significant difference between English and French gardens. The former reflected the power of agriculture and demonstrated the hegemony of large estate owners in English political and cultural life. The situation was otherwise in France. Under Louis XIV, power had been concentrated in the king at Versailles, expressed in the garden designs of Le Nôtre, where the perspective vistas seemed to extend infinitely. The picturesque garden in France developed during the years of political and economic turmoil under Louis XV and represented a reaction against architectural control. By mid-eighteenth century, surprise and amusement rather than noble simplicity were sought in French gardens. In a retreat to a romanticized rural life, gardens incorporated follies masquerading as dairies or other farm buildings, curved walks, asymmetrical plantings, and irregular terrain.

Benjamin Franklin arrived in Paris shortly after the Revolutionary War was declared in 1776, on a mission to entreat France's aid for the struggling colonies. When at leisure, he spent many delightful hours in the informal, English-style garden of the beautiful widow Madame Ligneville d'Helvetius in suburban Auteuil.[32] His taste for such gardens had been formed earlier in England through his friendship with Sir Francis Dashwood, who had improved his estate, West Wycombe in Buckinghamshire, with a lake, a cascade, groves of trees, and erotically suggestive garden buildings. Sir Francis, a founder of the Hell Fire Club, notorious for its debauched entertainments, included as

one of his garden decorations what he called Venus's Parlor, a cave that could only be entered through an oval opening between two outstretched banks. Franklin had written his son while staying there in 1775 that "the gardens are a paradise."[33] Like Sir Francis, he thoroughly enjoyed the society of women. While he lived in Paris, Franklin was embraced by everyone from courtiers to servants, working men to *philosophes*, despite his imperfect knowledge of the language, and among his countless friends—scientists, philosophers, and literary figures—were many attractive women who vied for his attentions.[34]

Franklin's own residence was in suburban

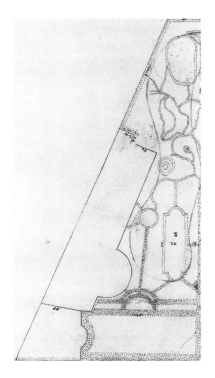

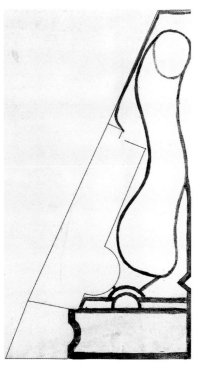

Passy at the Hôtel de Valentinois, where an old-style garden overlooked the Seine. The house was owned by a staunch supporter of American independence, Jacques Donatien Le Ray, and until 1779 Franklin lived rent-free in rooms opening onto a terrace overlooking the formal *potager* (vegetable garden) and orchard. Elkanah Watson visited Franklin there and recorded that "at the hour of dinner he conducted me across a spacious garden of several acres, to the princely residence of M. Le Ray." Here Watson was "enraptured with the ease and freedom" of the table conversation between the guests of both sexes.[35] Having been appointed ambassador, Franklin moved into one wing of the main house that centered on a grand formal parterre enclosed by hedges and decorated with classical sculptures. On a printing press in the garden of this first American embassy in the world, he ran off a daily paper in English and French for the information of expatriate Americans.[36]

Thomas Jefferson, who was appointed ambassador on Franklin's retirement in 1785, found a bounty of landscapes in the environs of Paris to feed his inquiring intelligence and instruct his taste. He frequented the Tuileries, the Bois de Boulogne, the Luxembourg Gardens, and the Jardin du Roi, where he presented the director, George-Louis Buffon, with a copy of his *Notes on the State of Virginia*. In the Bois de Boulogne, Jefferson noted Claude de Sainte-James's extravagant assemblage of picturesque structures and the *jardin anglais* of the comte d'Artois's estate Bagatelle with its romantic, if ephemeral, wooden temples, towers, and bridges lining a stream. Jefferson also knew Tivoli, a mock-rural estate in Paris, and presented its owner, Simon-Charles Boutin, with seeds from Virginia. Tivoli included an "anglo-chinois" garden with winding paths, an artificial river and cascade, groves, bridges, mounts, and a sheepfold.[37] Other gardening friends of Jefferson's included the comtesse de Tesse, who had a garden in the latest style at her estate, Chaville, and the duchesse d'Enville, to whom he gave seeds of Franklin's tree (*Franklinia alatamaha*) and tulip poplar, among other trees.[38]

Jefferson enjoyed an amorous flirtation with painter Maria Cosway, to whom he wrote the famous "Head and Heart" letter debating the wisdom of a liaison. During a day spent visiting gardens near Paris, Jefferson picnicked with

Maria at Marly, where they enjoyed the groves, vistas, and water features. Recalling the day, he exclaimed, "How beautiful was every object! … the gardens, the statues of Marly, the pavillion of Lucienne. Recollect too Madrid, Bagatelle, the King's garden, the Desert. How grand the idea excited by the remains of such a column!"[39] The Desert de Retz, recently laid out by François Racine de Monville, was a *jardin anglais* filled with picturesque structures and centered on a residence in the guise of a ruined column.[40]

Having visited gardens in the latest style in and around Paris, Jefferson was fortunate to find a residence where he could enjoy his own. In September 1785, he wrote Abigail Adams that "I have at length procured a house in a situation much more pleasing to me than my present…. It has a clever garden to it."[41] The house, on the corner of the rue de Berri and the Champs-Elysées, had been completed in 1778 and boasted a modern water closet. It occupied the corner of a generous, irregular-shaped lot that included a large *potager*. Here Jefferson grew American vegetables, including sweet potatoes and watermelons, and, as he informed a neighbor in Virginia, "I cultivate in my own garden here Indian corn for the use of my own table, to eat green."[42] He was perhaps affirming his American identity horticulturally, as he had done politically. The pleasure garden stretched back from the side of the property on the Champs Elysées and was separated from the tree-lined boulevard only by an iron grill, which made possible the visual incorporation of this borrowed view into the garden. Although Jefferson employed a full-time gardener, he himself drew three plans of the pleasure garden—one the original layout in the French picturesque interpretation of a *jardin anglais*, the two others somewhat simplified.[43]

Jefferson returned to America in 1789, but other Americans remained in residence during the French Revolution, most of them, like the merchant Thomas Handasyd Perkins, for trade. A few Americans, including Joel Barlow and Tom Paine, became involved with revolutionary politics abroad, as they had at home. Others, including Gouverneur Morris, who was known for his affability, wealth, and command of the French language, were immediately at home in French society. Morris shared a mistress, the comtesse de Flahaut, with Talleyrand and left a riveting diary recounting political events, social engagements, and his various amours.[44]

The end of the Napoleonic wars and the resumption of unhindered trade between America and Europe encouraged travel for pleasure. Paris became a goal; its charm and seductive way of life encouraged many Americans to settle there, for a season or for many years. For Americans with wealth and social ambition, residing in Paris could often open doors that were closed to them at home. The New York merchant Stephen Jumel unexpectedly married a noto-

Opposite top:
THOMAS JEFFERSON. Plan for the garden at the Hôtel de Langéac, c. 1785. Wash drawing on paper. The Huntington Library, San Marino, California

Jefferson's last Paris residence, the Hôtel de Langéac, is in the lower left. The courtyard and servants quarters occupied the large rectangle. The *potager* is not shown on the plan.

Opposite bottom:
THOMAS JEFFERSON. An alternate version of the plan, c. 1785. The Huntington Library, San Marino, California

This simplified plan reflects the English landscape gardens Jefferson had studied and would visit in 1786.

rious courtesan, Eliza Bowen, after keeping her in grand style for several years. Not surprisingly, Eliza was ostracized by hide-bound New York society, and so the Jumels sailed to France in 1815. Through a strange twist of fate, their vessel landed on the French coast near Rochefort, where the defeated Napoleon was frantically searching for means of escape. Their offer of ship transport reached Napoleon too late; he had already surrendered to the English. Nonetheless as a gesture of gratitude, he sent them an imperial carriage that held his campaign trunk and its contents.[45] When the Jumels arrived in Paris, their wealth, their confidence, and Napoleon's carriage guaranteed their acceptance in the highest circles. Jumel remained in France until the end of his life, but Eliza returned to New York in 1826, her social position assured by her triumphs in Paris.

A resident in 1836 reported, "The American society at Paris, taken altogether, is of a good composition. It consists of several hundred persons, of families of fortune, and young men of liberal instruction.... Americans at Paris are hospitable in a very high degree.... They form a little republic apart, and when a stranger arrives, he finds himself at home." He added, "One thing only is to be blamed. It becomes every day more the fashion for the elite of our cities to settle themselves here permanently."[46] American women traveling unaccompanied by a male relative felt safe in Paris. One recalled that "the Paris of 1869 was a city into which women might come at midnight, alone, unprotected, and not only be free from insult and imposition, but actually cared for, and sent to their rightful destination, in spite of their own ignorance and incompetence."[47]

By 1867 there were more than 5,000 Americans resident in Paris.[48] Many, like young Virginian Leonidas Polk Wheat, a student of piano and composition, sat out the Civil War there. Others, like James Gordon Bennett, the owner of *The New York Herald*, were fleeing scandal of one sort or another. A few even made careers there. Dr. Thomas W. Evans went to Paris in 1847 to practice dentistry and became a court favorite when his American skills brought him to the attention of Napoleon III. He returned the favor by helping the empress to safety in England in 1870.[49]

Equally successful was George A. Lucas, who had worked as an engineer in New York before leaving for Europe in 1857. He got no further than Paris, where he began a passionate affair with a Frenchwoman and fell in love with the city as well. He spent his first year buying works of art, which was the beginning of his subsequent career as an art dealer and advisor to American collectors such as William T. Walters of Baltimore. Lucas lived with his mistress (but in separate apartments) on rue de l'Arc-de-Triomphe, and in 1868 he bought a summer home at Boissise-la-Bertrand thirty miles from Paris. Here he gardened and supplied his French friends with seeds of the American corn that he grew.[50] Like Jefferson and so many Americans who followed, Lucas could not do without his corn on the cob. ◔

ITALY, THE CLASSICAL PAST

Before the American Civil War, Italy held the greatest romantic allure for traveling Americans. The classical world formed an integral part of the cultural fabric of the American colonies and the young Republic, not only through its literature, with which all educated persons were familiar, but in public buildings and imposing private residences that drew on its architectural vocabulary. The remnants of the classical world in Italy—the Greek temples at Paestum, the Greek and Roman sculpture in Florence and Rome, and the landscape itself, evocative of Horace or Pliny—drew a succession of American painters and sculptors, as well as the interested and adventurous who could afford the time and expense of an arduous European Grand Tour. As one American guidebook put it, "the history and literature of Rome are lying at our feet, and the living landscape is a page on which is written half of all we have learned at school and college."[51]

Benjamin West was one of the first American artists in Italy, arriving in 1760. West himself was a novelty to the well-traveled Europeans then living in Rome, and he was escorted on a tour of the famous monuments by a group of them eager to witness the reactions of this unsophisticated frontiersman from Pennsylvania. West gratified their expectations by exclaiming before the famous statue of Apollo Belvedere, "How like a Mohawk warrior!" In a more serious vein, he wrote to John Singleton Copley urging that he come to Italy, where he could "pursue the higher excellences in the Art, … the source from whence true taste in the arts have flow'd."[52]

JOHN SINGLETON COPLEY. *Mr. and Mrs. Ralph Izard* (*Alice Delancey*), 1775. Oil on canvas. Museum of Fine Arts, Boston, Edward Ingersoll Browne Fund, 1903, 03.1033

In this double portrait painted in Rome, Copley portrays the Izards, visiting from Charleston, South Carolina, as connoisseurs of the classical past, as was the artist. The Coliseum is visible in the distant landscape.

Copley took West's advice and went to Italy in 1774. In Florence he met Ralph and Alice Izard, a wealthy South Carolina planter and his wife, with whom he traveled to Paestum and the recently excavated Herculaneum and Pompeii.[53] Wealthy Americans, following the examples of their English counterparts, embarked on Grand Tours to the major cities, monuments and natural wonders of Europe, culminating in those of Italy. As a memento of their own Grand Tour, the Izards commissioned from Copley a double portrait full of the classical references that showed them to be people of taste as well as wealth.

Washington Allston, who rented an apartment overlooking the Spanish Steps in Rome from 1805 to 1808, was the first American to paint the Italian landscape, following the example of French painters Nicolas Poussin and Claude Lorrain, whose Arcadian visions had inspired the English landscape garden. Allston's friend Washington Irving was overwhelmed, as so many visitors were, by the "beautiful Italian scenery, palaces, and statues, and fountains, and terraced gardens." He wrote jealously of Allston: "He was to reside among these delightful scenes, surrounded by masterpieces of art, by classic and historic monuments, by men of congenial minds and tastes, engaged like him in the study of the sublime and beautiful. I was to return home to the dry study of law."[54]

Philadelphia painter Rembrandt Peale, who had been attempting to visit Italy since his first European trip in 1804, stated his longing in the most poignant terms: "The idea that my dreams of Italy were never to be realized, seemed to darken the cloud which hung over the prospect of death itself." He finally got there in 1829, at the age of fifty-one. His *Notes on Italy* brim with delight in the monuments he visited and the people he encountered. Attuned to traces of the past, he was charmed that in Tivoli, near Rome, "the visitor may see shops still in use, fashioned exactly like those of Pompeii." Although in the Boboli Gardens Peale missed the "charm of scenery which is produced by the picturesque manner of laying out the grounds in England," he was impressed by the "noble avenues of aged cypress and hemlock terminating in grand perspectives of fountains."[55]

Unlike Peale, many of these early visitors traveled with their wives and families, but few stayed long enough to establish a household or make a garden. Among the first permanent residents were a few American sculptors drawn to Italy by the skilled marble carvers and the congenial way of life

REMBRANDT PEALE. *Self-Portrait*, 1828. Oil on canvas. © 1986 Detroit Institute of Arts, Detroit, Michigan, Founders Society Purchase, Dexter M. Ferry Jr. Fund

Peale painted this portrait for his wife and left it behind when he went to Italy, not wanting his wife to forget him. He was away for two years.

possible there. As an American visitor in 1816 noted, in Italy "artists rank much higher in society than they do in other places."[56]

After sculptor Horatio Greenough graduated from Harvard in 1825, he was encouraged by Allston to go to Italy. In 1828 he arrived in Florence, where he studied sculpture and married Louisa Gore from Boston. Best known for his huge, semi-nude statue of George Washington, the first federally commissioned sculpture for the United States Capitol, Greenough made his living from portrait busts and Neoclassical figures, but he also wrote theoretical treatises on art and design. Following his own functionalist ideas rather than local traditions, he built a studio that included a "beautiful garden" noted by visitors.[57]

Two years before the Greenoughs returned to America in 1851, they moved from rented quarters in Florence to the Villa Brichieri at Bellosguardo, overlooking the Arno outside the city.[58] Horatio's brother Henry, a writer and architect married to the sister of the expatriate composer Francis Boott, visited there. A neighbor was the Boston portrait painter Francis Alexander, his wife, and their daughter, Francesca.

At Bellosguardo, Francis Alexander had begun to teach Francesca how to paint. After his death in 1880, his widow and his daughter chose to remain in Italy, where Francesca became a noted collector of Italian folk songs. She illus-

FRANCESCA ALEXANDER. *Charity*, 1861.
Oil on canvas. Private collection

Francesca Alexander dedicated her life in Florence not only to painting but also to work on behalf of the poor. The hill in the background may be Bellosguardo, crowned with its church.

LIZZIE BOOTT DUVENECK.
Villa Castellani, 1887.
Watercolor on paper. Iris & B. Gerald
Cantor Center for the Visual Arts, Stanford
University, California, gift of Francis and
Betty Duveneck

Francis Boott and his daughter lived
here together for many years until
Lizzie married American painter
Frank Duveneck in 1886.

Opposite: FRANK DUVENECK.
Portrait of Francis Boott, 1881.
Oil on canvas. Cincinnati Art Museum,
Cincinnati, Ohio

Duveneck painted Boott in the guise of
Titian's famous portrait of Renaissance
poet Pietro Aretino (Pitti Palace, Florence).

trated the songs with delicate drawings, which caught the attention of noted
English critic John Ruskin during one of his visits to Florence. Ruskin's gift
to her of a wild olive tree, dug up from the countryside, was the focus of her
terrace garden on the Piazza Santa Maria Novella.[59] Many years later, a visitor to this spot was surprised to find not only a real garden, but one that
reflected the New England origins of mother and daughter. "Their life in
those spacious rooms was naturally a good deal like their life in Salem had
been…. Everything in that Italian setting breathed out the strongest New
England atmosphere." In the garden, "growing in neat, diminutive beds of
earth there were flowers—flowers indubitably from Salem! Pinks, larkspur,
Shasta daisies, nasturtiums; ivy vines clambered over the gray stone parapet,
while in a corner to itself there was a tree, quite a big tree, beautifully
shaped, with vigor showing in every part of it."[60]

Francis Boott brought his young daughter, Elizabeth, from Boston to Italy to live after the untimely death of his wife in 1848. One wonders if he had read Henry Tuckerman's popular novel *Isabel or Sicily* (1839), in which the father of the eponymous heroine takes her to Italy after the death of his wife. Like Francis Boott, Isabel's father had eschewed worldly success for "faith in the refining influences of art." Bellosguardo had been recommended as a picturesque and healthful retreat by the Henry Greenoughs, so in 1855 the Bootts rented the Villa Castellani there. According to Henry James, who came for a visit in 1876, the Bootts' expatriation had done nothing but good for young Elizabeth, "this delightful girl, educated, cultivated, accomplished, toned above all, as from steeping in a rich, old medium." James noted that the Bootts "have a delightful old villa, with an immense garden and all sorts of picturesque qualities."[61] In fact, the Villa Castellani provided the model for Gilbert Osmond's house and garden in *The Portrait of a Lady*, which was written partly at Bellosguardo.[62] Unlike Pansy Osmond, however, Elizabeth Boott was to marry someone who did not measure up to James's standards of breeding and education, the American painter Frank Duveneck.

Most sculptors preferred to live and work in Rome. A visiting Bostonian, Thomas Gold Appleton, remarked in 1834 that "Rome is now a city of artists.... The galleries are full of them copying, and weeks may be spent visiting their studios."[63] One of Appleton's first calls was to the studio of Danish sculptor Bertel Thorvaldsen, where he found the garden a tangle of roses, mallows, broken statuary, and archaeological finds, a precedent for the gardens of resident American sculptors whose work was drawn from the classical past. By the 1840s, when wintering in Rome had become fashionable among well-traveled Americans, there were nearly one hundred American sculptors at work there.

Thomas Crawford arrived in 1835 to study with Thorvaldsen and in 1844 married Louisa Ward, sister of Bostonian Julia Ward Howe. His studio was picturesquely sited among the ruins

Harriet Hosmer and her workmen, 1867. Watertown, Massachusetts, Free Public Library

Diminutive sculptor Harriet Hosmer stands with her workmen in the courtyard garden of her Roman studio. Her *Fountain of the Siren* is in the niche behind her.

Top: The Palazzo Barberini, Rome. Mary E. Phillips, *Reminiscences of William Wetmore Story*, 1897

The garden along the via della Quattro Fontane had palm trees and flowers in island beds. William Wetmore Story and his family lived in a forty-room apartment here.

of the Baths of Diocletian, and his residence was on the second floor of the Villa Negroni, where the old gardens included a *potager*, fish pond, fountain, orange grove, cypresses, and a summerhouse.[64] After Crawford's untimely death, Louisa remained in Rome, where she married the American painter Luther Terry and moved with him and her three children into the Palazzo Odescalchi. On a visit in 1867, Julia Ward Howe noted "the whole of my modest house in Boyleston Place would easily, as to solid contents, lodge in the largest of these lofty rooms."[65]

Neither Louisa Crawford nor her oldest children returned to live in America, although she wanted her son Francis Marion Crawford, later a best-selling novelist, to be "a good American citizen." As Louisa Crawford's niece Maude Howe Elliott wrote, "her children grew up to be people without a country. The taproot was cut. They drew no nourishment from the land of their parents."[66] This was the case with children of many expatriate Americans. Sculptor William Wetmore Story sent his two sons to be educated in England; one of them followed his father's profession and occupied his studio in Rome, while his daughter married the Marchese Peruzzi di Medici. Story's studio had served as a model for that of American sculptor Kenyon in Nathaniel Hawthorne's novel *The Marble Faun* (1860), in which Hawthorne mused on the dilemma of expatriates. "The years after all have a kind of emptiness when we spend too many of them on a foreign shore.... Thus between two countries we have none at all."[67]

Story, a Harvard-educated lawyer, determined to become a sculptor after he traveled to Rome in 1847 to supervise the carving of a monument to his father. He remained there as he felt that "[i]t is of no use in America for me to hope for anything. I do not expect to find a public there until I have obtained it elsewhere."[68] In 1856 Story and his wife, Emelyn, moved into an elegant forty-room apartment in the Palazzo Barberini on the via delle Quattro Fontane. For nearly forty years the Storys were at the center of social and intellectual life, entertaining distinguished Italians as well as American residents, and such notable visitors as the poets Robert and Elizabeth Barrett Browning. The palazzo had gardens "of palm trees, flowers and fountains" but it was at Story's studio on the via San Martino that a visitor in the 1890s found the sculptor's own creation of "falling water in the court, a garden rich in vines, flowers and trees, and strewn with bits of old marbles, broken statues, a piece of cornice and frieze, a capital of curious carving, and other art fragments."[69]

The sculptor Harriet Hosmer had perhaps the most noteworthy American expatriate studio and garden, which was described in an 1869 guide as "a bijou of arrangement and decoration, quite unique in its kind in Rome or elsewhere."[70] Hosmer had gone to Rome from Massachusetts in 1852 and was accepted as a pupil by English Neoclassical sculptor John Gibson through the good offices of Story and the evidence of her own considerable talent for modeling and carving. After a year there, she wrote, "I wouldn't live anywhere else but Rome.... I can learn more and do more here, in one year, than I could in America in ten."[71] The large community of fellow artists, the availability of models, materials, and skilled workmen and above all the low cost of a comfortable life drew scores of women to study and work in Rome. Here they could live on their own, and as long as they maintained stringent standards of conduct, they were received cordially into the expatriate community.

Hosmer's sprightly personality and the appeal of her classical figures made her studio adjoining Gibson's a must for visiting Americans. Nathaniel Hawthorne noted there "a small orange tree in a pot, with the oranges growing on it, and two or three flower-shrubs in bloom."[72] By 1865 Hosmer was able to afford a studio built to her specifications, with nine rooms to accommodate all the workmen needed for each phase of production. The central feature of the courtyard garden filled with flowering shrubs was her 1861 *Fountain of the Siren*. A photograph taken in 1867 shows the diminutive sculptor in the garden surrounded by her workmen. ❧

CHARLES CARYL COLEMAN. *Il Pincio with
a View of Villa Medici*, 1888.
Oil on canvas. Berry–Hill Galleries, New York

PALAZZOS IN TOWN AND VILLAS BY THE SEA

Chapter Two

Steamships began plying the Atlantic in 1838, and by mid-century they were crossing weekly. After the Civil War, affluent Americans could travel to Europe in comfort and even luxury. Thousands with new fortunes joined those from old families who had long looked on European cities as less expensive and more attractive alternatives to American watering places. The daughter of one of these wrote, "My mother's family considered 'going to Europe' as the panacea for all evils, and were constantly in process of advance and retreat across the Atlantic."[1] Stays of a year or more were not unusual.

Italy offered a seductive climate as well as a vastly civilized way of life. Rome rather than Florence was now the destination of choice—as Boston journalist Lilian Whiting explained, "The social life in Rome is very brilliant, interesting and fascinating."[2] Henry James was ecstatic on his arrival in 1869 and exclaimed in a letter to his brother William, "At last—for the first time—I live! It beats everything; it leaves the Rome of your fancy—your education—nowhere.... I went reeling and moaning thro' the streets in a fever of enjoyment." James was bowled over not only by the "piazzas & ruins & monuments" but also by the feast for all the senses available there. During a later visit he wrote William that in Rome there was "a something that forever stirs & feeds & fills the mind & makes the sentient being feel that on the whole he can lead as complete a life here as elsewhere."[3]

Much of Roman social life was lived in the piazzas, the cafés, the public gardens, and the

Garden of the Palazzo Brancaccio, Rome, c. 1900. Country Life Picture Library, London

streets. It was James's habit to spend midday on the Pincian hill where "all the grandees and half the foreigners are there in their carriages, the *bourgeoisie* on foot staring at them and the beggars lining the approaches."[4] Crowning the Pincio was the Villa Medici, the seat of the French Academy in Rome, and beyond it the Villa Borghese, whose extensive grounds were open to the public. A visitor to the Villa Medici commented that "these formal rectangles and alleys are utterly shut in, so that in any one part one can see only the two dense green walls of box that enclose him and the glimpse of sky overhead.... This is the Italian idea of a garden."[5]

The garden of the Borghese was more expansive and included straight avenues lined with evergreen oak (*Quercus ilex*), a lake, three fountains, and the wooded glades in which Miriam and Donatello conduct their romance in Nathaniel Hawthorne's *Marble Faun*. Hawthorne felt that the Borghese garden was "more beautiful than the finest of English park scenery, more touching, more impressive, through the neglect that leaves Nature so much to her own ways... and the result is an ideal landscape, a woodland scene, that seems to have been projected out of the poet's mind."[6] For a generation brought up with a taste for picturesque landscapes, these overgrown gardens and Roman remains covered with vines were very appealing. American landscape painters in Italy in the middle of the nineteenth century had reinforced this vision with scenes of the Campagna and its moldering ruins.

A new garden made in Rome in the 1880s seems to have had these as models. Heiress Mary Elizabeth Bradhurst and New York merchant Hickson Field had traveled to Europe shortly after their marriage and remained there, eventually settling in Rome. In 1870 their only child, Elizabeth, married Prince Salvatore Brancaccio. At the end of that year, the American consul noted the simultaneous birth of a child to the Brancaccios and the flooding of their residence.[7] Wishing to establish their daughter and her family in more suitable surroundings, the Fields had a sizable villa built in 1880 in a natural park between the Coliseum and Santa Maria

Maggiore. The property included an old hunting lodge, Roman ruins, a lake, and ancient trees.

Mrs. Field was responsible for the garden, and she filled it to overflowing with trees, shrubs, flowers, and thousands of roses. She seems to have enthusiastically combined elements of the Mediterranean garden—terraces, paved areas, courtyards, fountains, and cypress—together with palms, cycads, and other exotics. A prominent feature of the garden was a ruined reservoir from 70 A.D. that had supplied water to the Coliseum and that she covered with roses and honeysuckle.[8]

Mary King Waddington, the American wife of a French diplomat, visited the estate in 1904 and described the garden: "You can't imagine anything more enchanting than that beautiful southern garden in the heart of Rome…. It is a paradise filled with every possible rarity of trees and flowers. It seems that whenever she saw a beautiful tree she immediately asked what it was and where it came from and then had some sent to her from no matter where. Of course hundreds were lost… but hundreds remain and the effect is marvelous. Splendid tall palms from Bordighera, little delicate shrubs from America and Canada all growing and thriving side by side…. There is a fine broad allée which goes straight down the winter garden to the end of the grounds with the Colosseum as a background. It is planted on each side with green oaks, and between them, rows of orange and mandarin trees…. It was too early for the roses, of which there are thousands in the season."[9]

Mary Waddington had lived in Rome as a girl in the 1860s, when her brother, Rufus King, was the United States minister to the Vatican. She recalled that in those days "young people came to Rome to educate themselves and enjoy the pictures, museums, historical associations." On her return to Rome twenty years later, she remarked on the daily ride taken by the fashionable set: "Now one saw nothing but American girls racing over the Campagna with a troop of Roman princes at their heels."[10]

A surprising number of these American women married into the Italian nobility, and Mary Waddington knew most of them, including Eugenia Berry from Georgia who married Prince Enrico Ruspoli. Eugenia, the daughter of a cotton factor and the widow of a wealthy businessman, began refurbishing the Ruspoli estate at Lake Nemi in 1901. Mary Waddington paid her a visit and noted the "beautiful garden under the walls of the castle."[11]

American dollars contributed to the restoration of other historic Italian residences, including the Palazzo Pamphili in Rome's Piazza Navona, the project of Francis Augustus MacNutt. MacNutt had grown up in Virginia and briefly attended Harvard, where he spent his weekends searching for colonial furniture and old china. In 1883 he left for Italy, where, he wrote ecstatically, "The enchantment of Rome gripped me and…I spent days visiting its wonders, absorbing its beauties, establishing contact with its spirit." He concluded: "my feeling was one of homecoming."[12] A convert to Roman Catholicism, MacNutt enrolled in the Accademia Ecclesiastica in Rome in 1888 and rapidly ingratiated himself into papal society, eventually becoming a chamberlain to the papal court. In 1898 he married heiress Margaret Van Cortlandt Ogden, whose brother and sister-in-law were expatriates in Cannes. Unlike other American residents who, as he wrote, "had not even troubled to learn the language" and paid no attention to either the classical past or "the artistic splendors of the Renaissance,"[13] MacNutt, who was fluent in Spanish, French, and German, as well as Italian, developed a passion for architecture, which found expression in his meticulous restoration of the palazzo to eighteenth-century grandeur.

G. P. A. HEALY. *Group of Artists in Rome*, c. 1869.
Oil on canvas. Illinois State Museum, Springfield

Rome was a Mecca for American artists until the 1870s. Healy shows landscape painter Frederick Church sketching the Arch of Titus, with Jervis McEntee and himself standing behind. Sculptor Launt Thompson is in the background, and beyond him is the Coliseum.

American artists were still drawn to Rome, and a few settled there. The painter William Stanley Haseltine, who had spent a student year in Rome, returned in 1869 with his second wife. They were cordially received into the community of American residents, which included the Storys, the Terrys, and the portrait painter G. P. A. Healy, who lived there with his wife and nine children before moving to Paris in 1877. The Haseltines rented a thirty-two-room apartment on the *piano nobile* of the Palazzo Altiere, which boasted a terrace one hundred feet long. Roses were Haseltine's passion, which he indulged on his terrace. Here a pergola was covered with jasmine and Banksia roses, and large terra-cotta pots were planted with palms and orange trees.[14]

Haseltine's three children first visited the United States on the occasion of the 1893 Chicago Exposition, when, according to his biographer, "last minute, hothouse attempts were made to force a sufficient amount of patriotism into bloom."[15] Like so many expatriates, however, Haseltine felt that his own residence in Italy had not made him less American. "Once an American, always an American: we are an original development totally unlike anything Europe has ever produced, even though every conceivable European element—Puritan, Cavalier, Huguenot, Catholic, nobleman, peasant, saint, and jail-bird—went into the making of us."[16]

In Rome an artist could live well on very little. In 1894 Maude Howe Elliott, a niece of long-time Roman resident Louisa Howe Terry, moved with her husband, painter John Elliott, into the upper floor of the Palazzo Rusticucci. She noted, "People who would be called well off at home are rich in Rome; people we should consider poor can live here with much comfort and some luxury."[17] Their comparatively modest apartment—an entry, salon, dining room, guest room, and master bedroom—overlooked St. Peter's Square and had a vast terrace, which Maude immediately began to fill with flowers. There was room for a fountain, orange trees, and a pergola where they dined. Her aunt Julia Ward Howe noted that Maude "delighted in the flowers of the terrace, which she called her hanging garden." On a visit in 1898, Julia Howe remarked on "the roses in their glory, red, white and yellow; honeysuckle out, brilliant."[18]

Maude Elliott rejoiced in the climate that made a year-round garden possible and frequently mentioned the flowers on her terrace in her memoir of life in Rome. In March 1895 she recorded wallflowers, daffodils, pansies, primroses, forget-me-nots, lilies of the valley, lilacs, and spirea in bloom and, in

Terrace garden of Palazzo Rusticucci drawn by John Elliott. From Maude Howe Elliott, *Roma Beata*, 1904

Like several other American residents in Rome, Maude Elliott had a notable terrace garden.

Top: Villa Crawford, Sant'Agnello di Sorrento. From Maude Howe Elliott, *Marion Crawford*, 1887

The garden of best-selling novelist Frank Crawford was on a cliff overlooking the Bay of Sorrento.

December 1897, white hyacinths, narcissi, pansies, and passion flowers. In midsummer 1900 she wrote: "The terrace is too lovely, ablaze with marigolds, cannas, cockscombs, balsams, oleanders, and passion flowers."[19] Like Francesca Alexander in Florence, Maude seems to have cultivated memories of New England gardens, as well as their flowers.

Maude Elliott became the biographer of her famous cousin, the prolific novelist Francis Marion Crawford, son of sculptor Thomas Crawford and Louisa Howe. Frank Crawford had grown up in Rome but attended boarding school in the United States before studying at Cambridge in England. His first best-seller, *Mr. Isaacs* (1882), was written in the garden of the summer house belonging to his aunt, Julia Ward Howe, and at Mr. and Mrs. Jack Gardner's estate in Beverly, Massachusetts. Isabella Stewart Gardner, fourteen years Crawford's senior, became his mentor and perhaps something more. He wrote to her about the book: "I think of it as someone else's work, as indeed it is, love, for without you I should never have written it."[20]

Crawford had developed a taste for writing in gardens. After he precipitately fled Boston and Isabella Gardner's attentions in 1883, he settled into a hotel at Sorrento, on the Bay of Naples. In its garden, according to Maude Elliott, he wrote five thousand words a day.[21] Crawford's subsequent Italian novels, particularly the Saracinesca trilogy set in the Villa Medici and its garden, have been credited with promoting the growing romance in America with the Italian garden.[22]

Crawford married Elizabeth Berdan, who had grown up in Europe, the daughter of General Hiram Berdan of Boston. In 1887 the Crawfords bought the Villa de Renzis, perched on the cliff edge at Sant'Angelo di Sorrento. Maude Elliott noted flowers, masses of roses, and fruit trees there, and a large terrace by the house for dining. The garden was decorated with several sculptures, as well as a Moorish fountain.[23] Here Frank Crawford continued his practice of writing out-of-doors, retreating to a nearby tower if visitors arrived. In 1899 he welcomed the visit of Henry James, who reported to Crawford's sister-in-law: "The beauty and splendor of this place are *invraisemblables*—the comfort and luxury ditto."[24]

The dramatic landscape and salubrious climate of the Bay of Naples drew many artists from Rome for excursions or permanent residence, among them American painters Charles Caryl Coleman and Elihu Vedder. After the Civil War, the two artists had shared a studio in Rome, which, according to a visitor, "opened on a beautiful garden full of orange and lemon trees, thick with vines." Vedder was particularly proud of the garden with its "ivy-clad walls and cypress trees and fountain."[25]

In the 1880s Coleman was drawn to the enchanting island of Capri in the Bay of Naples, which had remained without roads or tourists until ten years before he arrived. The island offered the painter dramatic landscapes and views of the sea, picturesque models in costume untouched by modern dress, and traces of the villas, gardens, and baths remaining from Roman times. This heady mixture furnished Coleman with an abundance of motifs for his popular paintings of young women in classical or peasant dress posed in the landscape or in gardens. Nostalgia for antiquity would affect his home and garden, as well as his paintings.

In 1886 Coleman bought an old convent overlooking the harbor in order, he claimed, to save "the most beautiful tree in the island," an ancient oleander.[26] The tree became the centerpiece for a series of garden rooms he gradually created in the courts of his Villa Narcissus. The entrance court held a pool for rainwater overhung by the oleander and decorated with Roman relief sculpture. Beneath an arch stood a copy of the Narcissus statue in the Naples Museum that had given the house its name. An inner courtyard had a marble stair cloaked with vines.[27] The courtyards were used as outdoor living rooms and decorated with trees in tubs and Roman antiquities from Coleman's impressive collection. Coleman later became as well known for his entertainments as for his paintings. A resident writer described him as "a splendid old dandy" and "a worshipper of what his generation called the fair sex," whose house was in the 1910s given up to "jolly parties with lots of good red wine."[28]

One of the young women taken under Coleman's wing was Romaine Goddard Brooks, who had been born in Rome of American parents. She went to Capri in 1899 as an impecunious young painter and lived there for several years in an

Charles Caryl Coleman's garden, Capri. Collection Paul Worman

In the terraced garden of his Villa Narcissus, Coleman trained vines on trellises and planted small trees and shrubs in pots.

Top: Charles Caryl Coleman and Rose O'Neill, Capri. Smithsonian Institution, Archives of American Art, Washington, D.C., Elihu Vedder papers

Illustrator Rose O'Neill created the popular Kewpie, whose success enabled her to buy Villa Narcissus in 1921.

abandoned chapel. She was adopted by the resident artists (Coleman was her "Uncle Charlie") and made a short-lived marriage to English writer John Brooks.[29] Having inherited a fortune, she returned to Capri in 1918 and two years later bought the spacious Villa Cercola, dispossessing Brooks, who had rented it for the duration of the war with E.F. Benson and Somerset Maugham. She replanted the neglected garden, adding flowers to the grapevines and olive trees.

Coleman enjoyed a more intimate relationship with Rose Cecil O'Neill, an illustrator notable for her creation of the Kewpie doll, a cross between a baby and an elf that became immensely popular. Rose O'Neill, with her husband, writer Harry Wilson, and the Booth Tarkingtons, had visited Capri in 1905 and been entertained by Coleman. After separating from Wilson, Rose returned in 1912 and resumed her friendship with Coleman, whom she rescued from financial disaster in 1921 by purchasing the Villa Narcissus and giving him life tenancy.[30]

Coleman had frequently painted in the garden of the neighboring Villa Castello, which was owned by two English painters, Sophie and Walter Anderson. In 1900 Detroit businessman Charles Lang Freer and his friend, scholar

CHARLES CARYL COLEMAN. *Garden of the Villa Castello, Capri*, 1906. Oil on canvas. © 1995 Detroit Institute of Arts, Detroit, Michigan, gift of friends of the artist

The Villa Castello was owned by Charles Lang Freer and Thomas Jerome. Its garden had groves of mature pine and cypress as well as flower beds and pergolas for vines.

Opposite:
CHARLES CARYL COLEMAN. *In the Shade of the Vines, Capri*, 1898. Oil on canvas. Private collection, courtesy Berry-Hill Galleries, New York

Coleman specialized in paintings suggesting the classical past. Incongruously, a new villa appears behind the women in Roman costume. Monte Solaro is in the background.

Thomas Spencer Jerome, acquired the Villa Castello. Freer had recently retired and would spend the remainder of his life traveling and collecting art, eventually endowing the Freer Gallery in Washington, D.C., in 1907. Jerome lived full-time on Capri and served as the American consul there while writing a history of Rome.[31]

Like Coleman, Freer and Jerome were inspired by the Roman remains on Capri in planning their grounds. Jerome titled his article on the villa "A Letter to Pliny the Younger," paying tribute to Pliny's famous descriptions of his Laurentian and Tuscan villas and gardens in his *Epistles*.[32] The entrance courtyard of Pliny's Tuscan villa had included four plane trees, and a portico overlooking beds of various shapes edged with box. A lower lawn was flanked with topiary animals and beyond it was a shrubbery with a circular walk enclosed in evergreens. Pliny's villa stood on high ground, but the Villa Castello's site was even more spectacular, at

CHARLES CARYL COLEMAN. *Villa Castello, Capri*, 1895. Oil on panel. Collection Graham Williford

This is the large pergola that stretched across the back of the Villa Castello garden.

the crest of Capri overlooking the Bay of Naples five-hundred feet below.

The drawing room of the Villa Castello was entered from a court planted with oleander, bamboo, a palm, and an orange tree, and the windows looked out onto a broad pathway through the garden flanked with laurel, fig, orange, lemon, and plum trees. There were two pergolas: a wide, columned one and another beyond with grapevines underplanted with wallflowers, geraniums, and nasturtiums. Unlike Pliny's garden, the grounds around the Villa Castello were full of flowers. Beds on either side of the large pergola were filled with pink mallows, Canterbury bells, snapdragons, geraniums, flax, and poppies. Jasmine, honeysuckle, and Banksia roses climbed columns and walls, and a round fountain was covered with calla lilies. Spirea, marguerites, iris, narcissus, sweet peas, pansies, lilies, and violets flourished between the garden trees. A hallway remaining from the Roman villa that had once occupied the site formed a grotto in the center of the garden dedicated to Bacchus and Venus.[33]

The Villa Castello was unusual in its relatively flat expanse, for most gardens on Capri clung to the hillsides, necessitating terraces on several levels. The garden that Coleman's friend Elihu Vedder and his wife made around their new villa on the side of the Anacapri mountain, christened the Tower of the Four Winds, was typical of many gardens in the area with no trees other than the ubiquitous olive. Vedder himself was the architect and designed a cubic structure on three levels with balconies and terraces that provided panoramic views of the Bay of Naples. The drawing room, library, and dining room opened onto a veranda, and on the second floor a hallway led onto a courtyard shaded by olive trees with a vine-covered pergola on one side. Another terrace a few steps up ended at Vedder's studio. The columns of the terraces were covered with climbers, and flowers in planters lined the steps and walls.[34]

The Vedders stayed in the house only in summer and continued to spend their winters in Rome. Vedder outlived most of his expatriate contemporaries—by 1894, at the formation of the American Academy in Rome, he was the grand old man of the American artists there. His Roman studio was near the Villa Mirafiori, to which the American Academy moved in 1897. The academy had an uphill battle attracting young artists to the residence program there, for by that date most preferred study at the Paris ateliers and academies.[35] The painter Frederic Crowninshield was the academy's director in 1909, when Clara Jessup Heyland donated the Villa Aurelia on the Janiculum Hill. In 1913 the academy merged with the American School of Classical Studies and moved into new headquarters next to the villa. Vedder, then eighty years

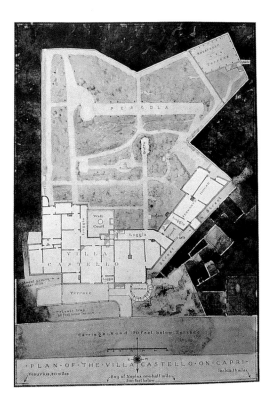

Fountain at Villa Castello on Capri. *House & Garden*, 1902

Plan of the Villa Castello. *House & Garden*, 1902

Bottom: A terrace at Torre Quattro Venti, Capri. Elihu Vedder papers, 1804–1969, Archives of American Art, Smithsonian Institution, Washington, D.C.

Vedder's wife and daughter sit on a terrace of his house overlooking the town of Capri.

Top: Garden of Torre Quattro Venti. Elihu Vedder papers, 1804–1969, Archives of American Art, Smithsonian Institution, Washington, D.C.

Vedder's garden was filled with flowers in raised beds and pots, and vine-covered trellises.

old, gave up his studio and donated his easels, worktables, and casts to the academy, marking the end of an era.[36]

Few American artists settled in Florence after the Civil War. One of these, Henry Roderick Newman, a landscape painter and member of the short-lived American Pre-Raphaelite group, had gone to Paris to study in 1870 but soon moved on to Florence. His studio and living quarters there were described by a visitor in 1884 as "unpretentious and refined" with Australian tree ferns, *Alocasia*, and arums in pots and the drawing room filled with flowers.[37]

Newman specialized in meticulously detailed watercolors of historical buildings and close-up views of wildflowers in natural settings. His paintings often included native anemones, daffodils, or iris, with branches of roses, olives, or grapevines in the foreground, as in his 1887 view of a villa on the hill at Bellosguardo. This is probably the Villa Montauto, where Nathaniel Hawthorne and his family spent the summer of 1858. It served as the model for Monte Beni, the ancestral home of Donatello in *The Marble Faun*.

William Merritt Chase, who famously remarked "I'd rather go to Europe than heaven," conducted summer painting classes for many years at his country home on Long Island. In 1907 he took his students to Italy, and during the trip he discovered the Villa Silli across the Arno from Florence, where it had a panoramic view of the city. The grounds included an olive grove, cypress and pomegranate trees, and an enormous oleander near the entrance of the villa. Enchanted, he rented it and was able to purchase it in 1910.[38]

Florence continued to appeal to American scholars and aesthetes, if not artists. Mabel Ganson Evans, a wealthy young widow from Buffalo, New York, arrived in Florence in 1905 with her new husband, Boston architect Edwin Dodge, and their young son. She had fled to Europe after the death of her first husband, seeking "a life made up of beautiful things, of art, of color, of noble forms, of ideas and perceptions about these.[39] She found an able collaborator, if not a satisfactory husband, in Dodge, and together they restored and decorated the Villa Curonia in Arcetri, near Florence.

Mabel herself planned the garden and described it with delight in her memoirs. No scholar, Mabel had nonetheless a general knowledge of Italian Renaissance architecture and decoration, as well as gardens. (*Italian Gardens*, written by the American architect Charles Platt and illustrated with photographs, had been published in 1897.) The grounds of the Villa Curonia already held old ilex, cypress, stone pine, and olive trees, together with oleanders, lilacs, and other flowering shrubs and box in abundance, but few flowers.

FREDERIC CROWNINSHIELD. *The Garden Wall, Villa Mirafiori*, c. 1900. Watercolor on paper. Stockbridge Library Association, Stockbridge, Massachusetts

The Villa Mirafiori became the residence of the American Academy in Rome in 1897 when Crowninshield was the director.

HENRY RODERICK NEWMAN. *The Villa di Bellosguardo*, 1887. Watercolor on paper. Private collection, courtesy Vance Jordan Fine Art, New York

During the previous autumn, which she spent on the Côte d'Azur, Mabel had noted
"flowers everywhere, climbing up the side of the house, scrambling over trees… flowers in
beds whose borders scarcely contained their unbridled out-pourings; too many flowers rudely
succeeding each other.… A perfect smother and riot of color and smell, too thick and heavy
and monstrous and multiple for delight."[40] At the Villa Curonia, Mabel would rely on trees,
shrubs, and vines. She had cypress planted along the drive with pink, single shrub roses and
purple iris in front, and she designed a formal garden at the west of the house, overlooked by a
loggia. Here lemon trees in terra-cotta pots on stone pedestals provided vertical accents in the
box-edged beds. Not sharing the Italian taste for bare exterior walls, Mabel had daphne, jasmine, and yellow climbing roses planted against the south wall, and yellow, pink, and white
Dorothy Perkins roses were trained on an iron pergola built before the library doors.[41]

From the entrance terrace on the north side, a crushed-brick pathway bordered with box
led to a stone bench. Mabel was so pleased with the effect of "the solid, dark green… bordering
the broad band of orange-pink" that she decorated the villa's entrance hall in those colors.

Villa Curonia, Arcetri. Beinecke Rare Book and Manuscript Library, Yale University, New Haven, Connecticut

Enormous terra-cotta pots of gardenias lined another walk that led along the base of the villa.[42]

Mabel became a noted if eccentric hostess, dressing in Renaissance-inspired costumes that echoed the decoration of her elegant rooms. Among her friends in Florence were Arthur Acton and his American wife, who had rented Villa La Pietra in 1903 and began planning a magnificent garden in Renaissance style with a green theater, terraces, and distant views of Florence.[43]

(Surprisingly, Mabel made no mention of this garden in her memoirs but noted that of Eugene Benson, a former tutor in Boston who had eloped with his employer, a Mrs. Fletcher, to Venice. They lived with her daughter, novelist Constance Fletcher, in the Palazzo Capello, where in the large garden, Benson "had tried to grow the sweet corn of Massachusetts."[44])

Acton was an English painter and art dealer who had grown up in Italy and studied at the École des Beaux Arts in Paris; he was also at one time an agent for the American architect Stanford White. In 1903 Acton had married Hortense Mitchell, the daughter of a Chicago banker; it was her inheritance that enabled them to buy La Pietra in 1907. The acquisition of such a property, which included fifty-seven acres containing productive vineyards and orchards, as well as an eight-acre garden, implied the assumption of patrician values and a way of life that was rapidly disappearing in

The Green Theater, Villa La Pietra, Florence. Curtice Taylor photograph

modern Italy. The original pleasure grounds of the villa had been remade as an English garden in the 1860s, but the garden Acton planned was a conscious reaction—the revival of formal, enclosed, and geometrically ordered spaces. Like other expatriates then occupying villas in the hills around Florence, Acton turned to Renaissance villas and gardens for inspiration. These villa owners sought the past, not modern Florence, which they looked down upon from a distance.[45]

The main axis of the Acton garden centers on the back of the villa with steps down from the door to a terrace with a basin in the center. A cross axis lined with evergreens leads to a *tempietto*, or small temple. From the next terrace, backed with a stone pergola, a cross axis leads to the Green Theater. This charming, semi-circular grass stage is fronted by box balls suggesting footlights and enclosed by wings of clipped yew. Such topiary theaters had been a feature of seventeenth-century Italian gardens. A splendid one at Villa Reale, Marlia, dating from 1652 has a grass stage eighty feet deep with topiary wings, backdrops, footlights, and a prompter's box. At La Pietra, as at Villa Reale, statues occupy the stage. On the lower lawn, a broken arch supported on Corinthian columns frames a view of the agricultural landscape and Florence beyond. A wealth of eighteenth-century sculpture animates the garden spaces.[46]

Until the 1860s Venice was considered unhealthy and avoided by many tourists, although the railroad had linked it with the mainland twenty years before. Writer William Dean Howells, the American consul in Venice during the Civil War years, complained of "the absolute want of society of my own nation in Venice."[47] Howells found the air of romantic decay that permeated the ancient Venetian palazzos most attractive. Indeed, the unkempt garden of the Palazzo Giustinani, glimpsed through an open door, had drawn Howells to live there, despite its lack of modern conveniences. He described the garden as "disordered and wild, but so much the better; its firs are very thick and dark, and there are certain statues, fauns and nymphs, which weather stains and mosses have made much decenter [*sic*] than the sculptor intended."[48] Howells's apartment was distinguished by high ceilings, stucco decoration, and Gothic windows that opened onto balconies overlooking the Grand Canal on one side and, on the other, a garden "full of oleanders and roses, and other bright and odorous blooms" kept by a neighbor.[49]

Venice became part of the new Kingdom of Italy when the Austrians withdrew from Lombardy-Venetia in 1866. The resulting collapse in property values meant that even expatriates of moderate means could afford to live in a palace. By the 1880s, there were increasing numbers of tourists and a score of Americans among the many foreign residents. In 1894

JOHN SINGER SARGENT. *An Interior in Venice*, 1899.
Oil on canvas. Royal Academy of Arts, London

Sargent was a cousin of the Curtis family, who are shown in their grand salon in the Palazzo Barbaro;
Daniel and Ariana Curtis are at the right, their son, Ralph, and his wife are at the left.

Henry James could complain, "Venice is full, the hotels overflow, and I meet every hour (that I am out) somebody I know of who knows me."[50]

Among these were Katherine de Kay Bronson, her husband, Arthur, and their daughter, Edith. Like many wealthy American couples, the Bronsons had spent an extended honeymoon in Europe and revisited the continent almost yearly from their home in Newport, Rhode Island. They decided to settle permanently in Europe in 1876, when they rented the Casa Alvisi on the Grand Canal. To one side of the house was a small courtyard filled with trees and flowering shrubs belonging to the Palazzo Giustiniani-Recanati. Wanting a garden, Mrs. Bronson rented a suite of rooms for guests in the palazzo. Her home became a refuge for scores of visitors, including her brother, New York publisher Charles de Kay, who wrote in her guest book: "The world's too feverish, hurried, clangorous—Wheels, and the vulgar, vex and frighten us!"[51] For de Kay and other visitors, the slow pace and lulling sounds of Venice's gondolas offered welcome relief from city bustle.

In 1880 Mr. Bronson abandoned his family for Paris, where he died five years later. Mrs. Bronson became a noted hostess, entertaining American and English residents, including the much-celebrated and recently widowed poet Robert Browning.[52] The poet lived with Mrs. Bronson for several months in 1888, and the following year he was a guest in her small house in Asolo, which was set into the city walls, with a garden on the hillside behind. Here Browning completed his collection of poems *Asolando*.

The Cortile of the "Garden of Eden." From Frederic Eden, *A Garden in Venice*, 1903

This enchanting garden, made by an English expatriate, was known to the American colony in Venice and was rented for several summers to Ralph Curtis. This courtyard just inside the entrance by the garden house was used for dining.

Browning gave the first public reading of this new book of poetry, dedicated to Mrs. Bronson, in the grand salon of the Palazzo Barbaro, the residence of Boston native Daniel Sargent Curtis, his wife, Ariana, and their son, Ralph. Daniel Curtis had left Boston under a cloud, having gotten into an altercation on a streetcar and ending up in jail. As he told the story, he had knocked down a man who had been insolent to his wife, a consequence of chivalry rather than choler.[53] He and his family lived in grand style in the Ca' Barbaro where one visitor found "flowering oleanders and palms along the steps and bowing gondoliers and Italian servants."[54] In 1894 Curtis was able to buy the palazzo from the Pisani family.

Henry James stayed with the Curtises for five weeks in 1887, finding them "most singular, original and entertaining." He returned in 1890 and when the Curtises lent the Palazzo to the Jack Gardners for the month of August 1892, he was again a guest there, sleeping in the library, a most sympathetic space. The Palazzo Barbaro caught James's imagination and served as the model for the Palazzo Leporelli in *The Wings of the Dove*, "where hard, cool pavements took reflections in their lifelong polish, and where the sun on the stirred seawater, flickering up through open windows, played over the painted...

ceilings." John Singer Sargent, a cousin of the Curtises, painted the family in the grand salon, as James described it, "all toned with time and all flourished and scalloped and gilded about."[55]

The Curtises' garden occupied the grounds of the Villa Vendramin on the eastern end of the Giudecca, the southernmost of Venice's islands and the most sparsely settled. The Vendramin grounds had the typical Venetian courtyard centered on a wellhead covering the cistern, with utilitarian gardens behind. Daniel Curtis noted in his diary on October 31, 1883: "Mr. Browning came to our garden Villa Vendramin, at the Giudecca, with his sister, and walked for an hour under the grape trellises." Henry James wrote that he often went with Mrs. Curtis to the garden late in the afternoon, and evidently thought it picturesque, as he urged her to show the garden and its garden house to visiting French writer Paul Bourget.[56]

The Curtis garden may have been something like the one on the Giudecca owned by Englishman Frederic Eden and described in his delightful book *A Garden in Venice*. (Eden's wife, Caroline, was the elder sister of Gertrude Jekyll, whose interest in gardening, however, dated to several years after the Edens made their garden.[57]) The Curtises, Bronsons, and other American residents were frequent visitors to the "Garden of Eden," as it was familiarly known.

The Eden garden began with a courtyard and a well, a hedged flower plot, and beyond this, pergolas for grapes bordering squares in which fruit trees were planted. Eden felt that "a brand new plan in the old ground was desecration," and he gave as much attention to restoring the pergolas and remaking the paths, surfaced with shells, as to the planting of the borders along the paths.[58] Eden discovered that the salt sea water was so close to the surface that only trees with laterally running roots would long survive—mulberries were a great success, as were many flowering shrubs, and of course figs. All the old-fashioned flowers flourished, among them daffodils, tulips, anemones, foxgloves, larkspurs, nigella, columbines, and roses by the hundreds. Eden wrote ecstatically: "No wonder that foreigners who have lived in Italy find it difficult to live out of it. There is the climate, the warmth, the beauty."[59]

Ralph Curtis rented the garden from the Edens for several summers before having his own on the Côte d'Azur.[60] He had married a wealthy widow, Lisa Colt, and hired the English architect Harold Peto to design his villa by the sea on Cap Saint-Jean, named Villa Sylvia after their first child. Peto was a friend of Henry James, who had introduced him in 1887 to Isabella Gardner, who, in turn, recommended him to Ralph Curtis.[61] The villa, built on a slope, was more Italian than French, with a recessed loggia connecting the two wings that opened out onto a terrace overlooking the garden. The natural features of the grounds, the olives, pines,

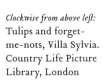

Clockwise from above left:
Tulips and forget-me-nots, Villa Sylvia. Country Life Picture Library, London

Ralph and Marjorie Curtis in the garden of Villa Sylvia, Cap Saint-Jean, France. Private collection

Terrace of Villa Sylvia. Private collection

Garden façade of Villa Sylvia. Private collection

and other natives, were retained and supplemented with magnolias, tree peonies, orange and lemon trees, and other flowering trees and shrubs. Crocus, narcissus, anemones, iris, and other bulbs lined the paths with pansies, violas, and annuals that were among the thousands of plants started from seed each year. On the south side of the house, a small loggia led into an enclosed garden of lushly planted geometric beds with a vine-covered pergola at one end.[62] The garden's relaxed layout and the luxuriance of trees, shrubs, and flowers allowed to grow as they might was unlike Peto's later designs and seems to have reflected the taste and artistic training of Ralph Curtis himself.

Bernard and Mary Berenson visited from their villa, I Tatti, outside Florence and reported to Isabella Gardner on the success of the Curtis garden and its floral splendor. In 1911 Berenson wrote: "The garden is a dream of loveliness. Between Ralph's taste and attention and the incredible willingness of the soil and climate, floral miracles are performed daily." The next year Mary Berenson exclaimed, "What a lovely, what an enchanting garden they have made there at the Villa Sylvia! I have just sent my own gardener there to see what a garden can be...[he] only knows the *uso italiano*, which does not include flowers."[63]

The floral splendor of Villa Sylvia impressed Harriet Martineau, who featured it in her *Gardening in Sunny Lands* (1924). She enthused that "the azure Mediterranean glints happily through borders of purple iris, and glades of emerald turf shaded by ancient olive trees lead on to a fairyland of flowering shrubs." She noted inventive combinations—tree peonies under olives, spirea under prunus, drifts of white iris and scarlet anemones under cherries, blue echium with white broom. Paths and steps were lined with nasturtiums, orange nemesia and marigold, freesia, crimson cyclamen, and black ranunculus. On the top terrace, masses of heliotrope and purple stock glowed against the bougainvillea covering the villa.[64]

FREDERICK CARL FRIESEKE. *Lilies*, c. 1912.
Oil on canvas. Terra Museum of American Art, Chicago.
Courtesy Berry-Hill Galleries, New York

ARTISTS' GARDENS IN FRANCE AND ENGLAND

Chapter Three

In post–Civil War America, a young man or woman who wanted to become an artist had limited options for training and scant encouragement. New York, Philadelphia, and Boston had noted art schools and a critical mass of interested patrons, but they were the exception. The Mecca for aspiring artists was Paris, with its ateliers, academies, annual Salons, and booming art market. Women were not admitted to the state-run and tuition-free École des Beaux Arts there, but training was available either in the ladies' classes at the Académie Julian or in the studios of noted French masters. During the summer, while the academies were closed, art students flocked to the countryside for landscape and figure painting out-of-doors.

In the 1860s and 1870s, the forest of Fontainebleau was the destination of choice, because the French Barbizon painters enjoyed a tremendous vogue in the United States. By the 1880s, with the growing acceptance of Impressionism, knowledgeable students had developed a taste for more open landscapes and for color in a higher key. In 1876 a group of English and American students discovered the village of Grez-sur-Loing, about forty miles south of Paris with a charming old stone bridge, red-roofed houses, enclosed gardens, and a quietly flowing river. The two inns at Grez rapidly filled with artists, whose close association offered not only camaraderie but also freedom from convention. Even so, Philadelphia painter Alexander Harrison must have caused a stir when he posed his nude models in a garden there. Nevertheless, the success of his lush *In Arcadia*, depicting four women in dappled light under the willows, at the Paris Salon in 1886 gave legitimacy to the plein-air painting of nudes.[1]

Romance as well as friendship was fostered in the casual atmosphere of Grez. The Boston painter Francis Chadwick met a Swedish sculptor, Emma Lowstadt, at the Hôtel Chevillon. They married in 1882 and settled in Grez, first in a house subsequently occupied by the composer Frederick Delius, and later in the former Hôtel Laurent. Both of these houses had significant gardens that were favorite spots for painting. Canadian painter William Blair Bruce met Swedish sculptor Caroline Benedicks at the Chevillon, and they returned frequently to Grez after their marriage in 1888. In this painting by an unknown artist, it may be either Caroline Benedicks or Emma Lowstadt depicted at work in the hotel garden, along with a woman painter and two onlookers.[2]

Another Boston painter, Robert Vonnoh, brought his new bride to the Hôtel Chevillon in 1886 and returned the following year. Vonnoh appreciated the Chevillon's enclosed garden laid out in terraces down to the river, its bordered beds filled with vegetables, flowers, grapes, figs, and peaches. He was to spend much of the next four years there, producing vibrant plein-air landscapes, as well as several large paintings destined for the Salon that would establish his reputation back home. Vonnoh returned to Boston in 1891 to pursue a career as a portraitist, but landscape remained his first love.

In Chicago for the World Columbian Exposition of 1893, where his paintings were featured, Vonnoh met Bessie Potter, a petite, vivacious young woman and a gifted sculptor. After his wife's death in 1899, Vonnoh married Bessie and took her to live at his cottage in Rockland Lake, New York, where his passions for both gardening and landscape painting flourished. It was not until 1907 that Vonnoh was able to return to France; he rented a house at Grez, where he spent time each year until the outbreak of World War I. (Bessie was not as enthusiastic about Grez, objecting to the lack of modern plumbing, and she often lingered in New York.) In the long, narrow space behind the house at Grez, Vonnoh managed to grow both flowers and vegetables.

UNKNOWN. *Group of Artists in a Garden, Grez-sur-Loing*, c. 1885–95. Oil on canvas. Ball State University Museum of Art, Muncie, Indiana, gift of the Edmund Burke Ball heirs, 1986.041.12

This garden may be that of the Hôtel Chevillon, which was frequently used as an outdoor studio.

Robert Vonnoh in the courtyard of his house in Grez-sur-Loing. Courtesy Mrs. Robert Rowe Thompson

The narrow garden behind Vonnoh's house was filled with flowering shrubs, vines, and flowers as well as vegetables, including his favorite sweet corn.

He made a wide border along the path to the river for his favorite annuals, planted flowering shrubs near the house, and trained hollyhocks and vines over the fence that enclosed the vegetable plot. Perhaps in a moment of homesickness, he sent an urgent card to New York in March 1909 urging Bessie to "[c]all up Henderson & get him to send me at once a packet of sweet corn, not Country Gentleman, but the best large kernel that might succeed in France in a favored location.... Ask him to send me his catalogues as well & pay him what it costs & make sure he sends it at once."[3]

As Impressionism and outdoor painting in general gained acceptance, American artists in France found a garden a great convenience, if not a necessity. Portrait painter G. P. A. Healy, who had lived for several years in Rome, moved in 1873 with his family to Paris, where he leased the house and studio recently vacated by Frederick Winterhalter, the noted society portraitist. One of Healy's nine children recalled that the house was separated from the studio by "a garden of about twenty feet by one hundred feet with age-old trees."[4] Healy used the garden for receptions and as an outdoor portrait studio.

Expatriate Daniel Ridgway Knight, who specialized in paintings of young peasant women posed in the countryside or in gardens, had a special glass-enclosed studio built in his garden at Poissy for painting in outdoor light. An American colleague wrote enviously, "Here the artist can work in all weathers except the warmest, and in the winter, with the snow upon the ground, is able to sit comfortably and finish pictures commenced in summer."[5]

James Abbott McNeill Whistler first went to Paris in 1855 to study, and then he moved on to London, where he became a leading painter of the Aesthetic Movement. However, Paris, then in the forefront of modern painting, eventually proved a more congenial and stimulating environment. Whistler visited frequently and, in 1892, moved with his wife, Beatrix Godwin,

JAMES McNEILL
WHISTLER.
The Garden, 1891.
Lithograph on paper.
(One of six proofs
from the Way edi-
tion.) Collection
Steven Block

Whistler's garden
at 110, rue du Bac,
Paris, was used for
entertaining as well
as sketching.

JAMES McNEILL
WHISTLER.
*Confidences in the
Garden*, 1894.
Lithograph on paper.
(One of twenty-eight
proofs from the Way
edition.) Collection
Steven Block

to a garden apartment at 110, rue du Bac near the Luxembourg Gardens. Beatrix used the garden for entertaining, but for her husband it was an outdoor studio for portraits of his family and friends.[6] Here he sketched a group assembled for tea that included fellow painter Walter Sickert with Beatrix Whistler and her sister Ethel. Another visitor was Henry James, who took note of the little garden house built into the wall. The other furnishings were suitably aesthetic and included a rattan plant stand, a metal folding table with side chairs, and two wooden seats with lattice arms and backs.

Whistler's garden served Henry James as a model for that of the sculptor Gloriana in *The Ambassadors* (1903). In the novel, a poignant dialogue during Gloriana's garden party between New England-bred Lambert Strether and aspiring artist Little Bilham was based on an incident related to James by his friend Jonathan Sturges, who had been to tea in the Whistlers' garden with William Dean Howells in 1894. The cautious and conscientious Strether, deeply moved by the cultivation and nuance of life in Paris, echoes Howells's words: "Live all you can; it's a mistake not to.... I see it now. I haven't done so enough before—and now I'm too old."[7]

Knight, Whistler, and many other expatriate painters never returned to America. As one writer on American art explained at the time, those who chose to return home were often at a disadvantage. "Obliged to stand on their own feet, no longer sustained by competition, technical advice, and by the suggestions derived from artistic surroundings, absolutely alone, without even sympathy, generally forced to earn their living as artisans or in some branch of art unsuitable for them…they long for the artistic atmosphere of Europe."[8]

Beginning in 1886, a group of American painters congregated at the Hotel Baudy in Giverny, forty miles northwest of Paris. Claude Monet had settled in Giverny in 1883, but the first Americans there claimed not to know he was in residence. The spectacular flower garden in front of his house, however, soon received much attention in the American press. In 1889 Lilla Cabot Perry arrived with her husband and three daughters. The Perrys had moved from Boston to Paris two years earlier so that Lilla could study painting. After settling in Giverny, she became an early supporter of Monet and promoted his paintings in the United States.

In 1894 the Perrys rented Le Hameau, two small cottages next to Monet's home where he would occasionally join them in their garden to smoke his postprandial cigarette.[9] A later tenant was Mary C. Wheeler, director of the Wheeler School in Providence, Rhode Island, who brought a group of young women to France every year for painting instruction. One of them later described the garden: Between the two cottages was "a grass plot shaded with plum trees, walnut trees, and a large horse chestnut" and beyond was the garden proper, with "rose trees, flower beds and the pool."[10] Unlike Mary Wheeler's students and later American arrivals, Lilla Perry preferred to paint in the open countryside rather than in the garden. Monet himself did not paint his flower garden until 1900, although he had begun a water-lily series three years before.[11]

Garden painter Blondelle Malone from Columbia, South Carolina, spent the summer of 1904 in Giverny. Unlike most American residents, she managed to break through the formidable barriers Monet had erected to preserve his privacy. She reported: "He refused to see everyone—especially Americans and artists. Fifteen years ago they came here and almost drove Monet wild. They would come into his garden, which is wonderful, uninvited, run over his place and imitate his painting." Attractive, vivacious, and fluent in French, Blondelle managed to elicit a critique from the master.[12]

Another young American woman who had been at the Académie Julian in Paris, Mariquita Gill, arrived with her mother in 1891 and the following year rented a house where they lived for the next six years. Mariquita Gill was an avid gardener and filled the border along her garden path with lilies, roses, hollyhocks, and poppies that were the subjects of many paintings, such as *Lilies*, which shows the flowers against the garden wall underplanted with poppies. Lilies, especially white Madonna lilies, were favorite subjects for garden painters. Not only

FREDERICK MACMONNIES. *Mrs. MacMonnies, Betty and Marjorie*, 1901.
Oil on canvas. Musée des Beaux Arts, Rouen

In the MacMonnies garden at Giverny, beyond the shelter of clipped
lindens where the family sits, there was a narrow terrace draped
with grapevines.

Opposite: MARY FAIRCHILD MACMONNIES. *Blossoming Time*, 1901.
Oil on canvas. Union League Club, Chicago

The lower garden had an orchard, *potager*, pool, and flower beds
along the walls.

were they statuesque and beautifully formed, but
they also suggested a range of references from
purity and virtue to the Aesthetic Movement's
idea of art for art's sake.

Mariquita Gill's garden was used by at least
one other American artist. Impressionist
Theodore Robinson noted in his diary on October
30, 1892: "Worked a.m. in Gill's garden with
Yvonne on Large Layette."[13] Robinson's diary
also noted that on October 9, he had attended
a tea given in honor of Mariquita's engagement
to Arthur Murray Cobb, a painter from New
York. They married the following year but were
divorced in 1895.[14] Interestingly, this episode was
not mentioned in the memorial biography of
Mariquita commissioned by Mrs. Gill after her
daughter's untimely death in 1915.

New American arrivals in Giverny tended
to choose gardens rather than the surrounding
countryside as settings for their work. Sculptor
Frederick MacMonnies and his wife, Mary
Fairchild, a painter, first arrived in Giverny in
1890. In 1895 they rented a cottage with a well-
kept garden, where Mary MacMonnies painted
Roses and Lilies, a vibrant self-portrait with her
young daughter against a background of bloom; the picture was awarded a gold medal when it
was shown at the 1900 Exposition Universelle in Paris.

In 1898 the couple bought Le Moutier, a converted priory familiarly known as the
MacMonnastery. Frederick MacMonnies, an ardent womanizer both at home with his young
women pupils and abroad, was in residence only in the summer. Mary MacMonnies spent most
of the year there with her two daughters and developed a passion for gardening. She described
Le Moutier in her unpublished memoirs as "a place that had grown and developed during two

hundred years or so…surrounded by solid stone walls ten feet high, insuring discretion. Long paths between rows of fruit trees and of grape vines…vegetable garden and barnyard, lawns and flower beds. This became my own beautiful plein air open-air studio." Through daily consultations with the hired gardener about "pruning, planting, fertilizing, spraying, and…many other details of which I knew nothing," Mary gained, as she put it, "a liberal education." She added: "I took a lively interest in these matters and became quite expert."[15]

Frederick also took an interest in the garden. A visitor in 1901 noted that "MacMonnies has taught his French gardener to grow corn and other vegetables peculiar to his native country," and claimed that the garden was "the most beautiful, the most picturesque and artistic" in Giverny, surpassing even that of Monet.[16]

The garden was laid out on three levels, with meandering gravel paths bordered in box. The upper terrace, shaded by a chestnut, was centered on a circular pool with a statue of Pan in the center. Along the low stone wall backing the terrace stood copies of the Diana, Narcissus, and the Dancing Faun statues discovered at Pompeii. Below, a narrow parallel terrace was covered with a grape arbor. At one end of the terrace was the enclosure of clipped lindens where Frederick painted Mary with their two daughters and a nurse. Steps led down to a

MARY FAIRCHILD
MACMONNIES.
Giverny Garden, c. 1900.
Oil on canvas. Sheldon
Swope Art Gallery, Terre
Haute, Indiana

The pool with its statue
of Pan centered the upper
terrace of the garden.
Beyond the wall the grapevines on the second terrace
catch the sunlight.

large enclosure with flowers and fruit trees in rectangular beds along the wall, a decoratively
arranged vegetable plot, and a lawn surrounding a stone pool. Among the flowers were poppies,
roses, lilies, dahlias, and self-sown forget-me-nots.[17]

Mary painted the garden in all seasons—a glorious view of the lower garden in spring
when the cherry trees were in bloom, the upper garden in summer, and in the winter under
snow—and also made nude figure studies there. As she noted in her memoirs, the high walls
insured discretion. Other visiting artists used the garden for plein-air figure painting, both
clothed and nude. One of these, William de Leftwich Dodge, arrived in 1898 with his family.
By this date, as his daughter remarked, "The per capita population of garden nudes in Giverny
was becoming extraordinary, even in France." She gleefully recalled that a nude Parisian
model once opened the garden gate expecting an artist neighbor, but it was instead a
Presbyterian minister visiting from Virginia.[18]

In 1901 Will Hicok Low and his wife were guests of the MacMonnies for several months.
Mary painted Mrs. Low standing by the upper garden basin, and Will Low painted several views
of the garden. He was impressed not only with the garden but also with the garden's mistress;
after his wife's death and Mary's divorce from Frederick in 1909, the two painters were married.[19]

The painter in Giverny most noted for plein-air nudes was Frederick Frieseke from
Michigan, who first stayed at the Hotel Baudy in 1905. He married that autumn, and the fol-

KARL ANDERSON. *Portrait of Frieseke Painting*, 1910. Oil on canvas. Private collection

Frieseke specialized in paintings of women in sunlight, both nude and clothed. His garden in Giverny served as an outdoor studio.

Below: WILL HICOK LOW. *The Terrace Wall*, 1901. Oil on canvas. Albany Institute of History and Art, Albany, New York

The flower-bordered wall held copies of Pompeian sculpture.

lowing summer the Friesekes rented a house from Mme. Baudy. A later visitor described "high walls on three sides, a two-story cottage on the fourth, while the garden is a riot of flowers, vines and trees."[20] Here the Friesekes would spend the summer months, returning to their Paris apartment for the winter. The garden sloped down to a stream and pond, where Frederick often posed his nude models in the dappled shade of the willows.[21] Although he also painted figures in interiors, the garden was essential to his work. As he revealed to a visitor, "it is sunshine, flowers in sunshine, girls in sunshine, the nude in sunshine, which I have been principally interested in."[22] His passion for light, brilliant color, and decorative patterning was nourished by the planting of the garden, which was planned and tended by his wife, Sadie.

Green lattices were attached to the garden walls and one side of the stone cottage to hold roses, clematis, and passion flowers. A border between the cottage and the box-edged path held

FREDERICK CARL FRIESEKE. *The Garden*, 1915.
Oil on canvas. Private collection, courtesy Berry-Hill
Galleries, New York

A circular pool was the focus of the grass area by the
house. Branching paths bordered in box led further
into the garden.

white lilies and iris, and the narrow border on the other side of the path was planted with low annuals. An axial path bordered with dahlias led to a circular pool, where it divided into three, forming irregularly shaped beds for lawn and flowering shrubs and soft fruits, as well as flowers. Along the garden wall, beds held acanthus, snakeroot, mullein, foxglove, hollyhocks, and other majestic plants.

Much of the Friesekes' daily life was lived outside. A niece who visited in 1910 recalled, "It was our custom to spend a great deal of time in the garden. Sadie would usually read aloud while Fred painted.... I can close my eyes now and see them against the tall spikes of delphinium and the big pink roses. Around them were clumps of sweet william and daisies yellow and white; there were also marigold, calendula, campanula, and snapdragon. The poppies and lilies were through blooming; but the hollyhocks, shading from pale yellow through deep scarlet, made a tapestry of radiant colours."[23]

Unlike most of the American residents, the Friesekes had become acquainted with Monet; Sadie spoke excellent French and could talk knowledgeably with him about horticulture. Her niece reported that Monet "liked Sadie, and he wanted her to be one of the first to see a little bridge just completed"—his new water-lily garden and its Japanese bridge.[24] Monet's gardens must have been thrilling, with their lush planting and glowing colors. In the garden before his house, arranged in a grid from a central axis, perennials were planted in large blocks with climbing vines and roses for vertical accents and brilliant annuals such as nasturtiums filling in the edges of beds. His water-lily garden held iris, gunnera, peonies, azaleas, and wisteria. Monet employed five gardeners; Sadie just one.

Frederick Frieseke chose to remain in France with his family during World War I in order to keep painting. As he explained, "I stay on here because I am more free and there are not the

FREDERICK CARL FRIESEKE.
The Fountain, 1923.
Oil on canvas, Private collection

Frieseke's wife, Sadie,
sits beside the pool in the
Normandy garden. The
boy and frog fountain is
by Janet Scudder.

Below: Frieseke house and
garden, Normandy, 1939.
Collection Nicholas Kilmer

The Friesekes moved in 1920
to this stone and half-timbered
house and re-created their
Giverny garden on a smaller
scale. Box-bordered beds in
front of the house held annuals.

Puritanical restrictions which prevail in America. Not only can I paint the nude here out of doors, but I can have a greater choice of subjects."[25] After the war, the Friesekes moved to a stone and half-timbered farmhouse in Mesnil, Normandy. The garden was laid out in ascending terraces with an axial path that led from the door of the dining room, circled a small pool, rose by stairs to another terrace where there was a cutting garden, and climbed again to an old linden allée at the crest of the hill. On the first terrace there were box-edged beds and a yew clipped into the shape of a basket. On the second were beds for flowers, including primroses, roses, nasturtiums, lavender, and marguerites. Roses and clematis were trained against the house.[26]

These painters' gardens, enclosed by high walls or hedges and filled with flowers, shrubs, and cloaking vines, could not help but reflect a change in the mode of perceiving the landscape itself. As we have seen, late-seventeenth-century paintings by Claude and Poussin, with their high vantage points, carefully framed vistas, and orderly progression into the distance, had a demonstrable effect on the English landscape garden of the 1700s. At the beginning of the 1800s, taste turned away from grand vistas and history painting in favor of more emotionally charged, romantic scenes in art and to picturesque landscapes characterized by complexity, irregularity, strong contrasts of light and shade, and varied surfaces. Mid-century gardens erupted with brilliant beds of annuals, myriad flowering shrubs, and specimen trees dotted about. At the end of the century, intimate forest interiors or closed-in, close-up views appeared in landscape painting. Gardens turned inward; the experience was one of immersion, as in an Impressionist painting.

The Frieseke gardens in both Giverny and Normandy can be seen as well in the context of revivalist gardens that had become newly fashionable both abroad and in the United States with the Colonial Revival. In France there was renewed interest in Renaissance gardens; for example, at the Renaissance Château Villandry on the Loire, Joachim Carvallo and his American wife, Ann Coleman, beginning in 1906 replaced a *jardin anglais* and arabesque beds of annuals with a spectacular box-edged *potager* (decorative vegetable garden), parterre garden, and grand *basin d'eau* (pool) based on seventeenth-century prototypes.[27]

JOHN SINGER SARGENT. *Self-Portrait Painting "Carnation, Lily, Lily, Rose,"* 1885. Pen and ink. Francis Davis Millet and Millet family papers 1858–1984, Archives of American Art, Smithsonian Institution, Washington, D.C.

Sargent painted *Carnation, Lily, Lily, Rose* during a few minutes of twilight each evening over the course of two summers.

In England, the Arts and Crafts Movement had espoused gardens on a smaller scale with the cottage garden as a model. As has often been pointed out, the cottage garden was a nineteenth-century invention, the creation of middle-class nostalgia for a romanticized bucolic past. The popularity of the cottage-garden style, with its box-edged beds overflowing with old-fashioned flowers, was symptomatic of a revival of interest in old British gardens from the medieval *hortus conclusus* (enclosed garden) to Tudor topiary led by Arts and Crafts practitioners such as William Morris. The cottage garden also evidenced a reaction against the use of tender annuals in bedding-out schemes of carpet beds and ribbon borders inveighed against by both English and American garden writers.[28] In an Arts and Crafts garden, the integration of house and garden was accomplished by an architectural garden structure. Clipped hedges divided the garden into a succession of discrete spaces filled with beds and borders, edged with box and often accented with topiary figures.

In 1885, nostalgia for a romanticized past led the American painter Francis Davis Millet and his wife, Lily, to settle in England at Broadway,

Worcestershire. Francis Millet had begun his career in Boston and gained renown for his paintings of eighteenth-century life, a reflection of the Colonial Revival then in the ascendant in America. He had gone to England in search of the visible past for his historical work and was advised to try Broadway, both for its own charm and for its proximity to Shakespeare's Stratford-upon-Avon. Earlier, William Morris had stayed in the eighteenth-century crenellated Broadway tower and given the village his imprimatur as "a work of art."[29]

The Millets rented a house on the green, where they were joined by their friends the American illustrators Edwin Austin Abbey and Frederick Barnard and the English garden painter Alfred Parsons, who was noted for his illustrations for the 1881 edition of William Robinson's *The Wild Garden*. The artists companionably shared living quarters and expenses. John Singer Sargent arrived in August and took up residence in a nearby inn, the Lygon Arms. Needing more space, the Millets bought the adjacent former priory, which they christened "Abbot's Grange," and began restoring it to medieval splendor. On a visit in 1886, Henry James was given a writing room there.[30]

Abbey and Millet shared the large barn studio, where Abbey stored his extensive collection of antique costumes. Sargent painted in the garden and began a fresh canvas each morning, painting exactly what he saw. Indeed, much of the garden

JOHN SINGER SARGENT. *Carnation, Lily, Lily, Rose*, 1885–86. Oil on canvas. Tate Gallery, London

The setting is the garden of Frank and Lily Millet at Broadway, Worcestershire.

JOHN SINGER SARGENT. *Francis Davis Millet's House and Garden*, 1886. Oil on canvas. Berry-Hill Galleries, New York

The garden at Russell House is seen at the beginning of the Millets' residence, with lilies in pots and a few roses.

developed in the course of outdoor painting there. In 1885 the residents wanted to paint poppies, so they grew a great bed of them. The following summer, Sargent saw at a nursery a half-acre of roses in full bloom and bought them all to paint.[31]

Sargent's garden studies led to the magnificent *Carnation, Lily, Lily, Rose*, which he began in August 1885 and finished the following summer, working rapidly each evening while the twilight lingered. ("Carnation, Lily, Lily, Rose" was the refrain of a song popular that year, as well as a reference to the depicted flowers.) Sargent complained of the practical and aesthetic difficulties involved in this painting: "There are hardly any flowers and I have to scour the cottage gardens and transplant and make shift.... Impossible brilliant colors of flowers and lamps and brightest green lawn background. Paints are not bright enough and then the effects only last ten minutes."[32]

Francis Millet's sister Lucia forced twenty lilies in pots for the picture and planted thirty additional bulbs, sent by Sargent, to bloom in 1886. The garden was greatly improved in that year with the purchase of the neighboring Russell House, which had a gazebo, a tower with greenhouse, an orchard, a lily pond, and woodland.[33] Most of the roses were planted within the walled garden there. Eventually Lily and Lucia Millet pulled it all together into a splendid display of old-fashioned flowers in Arts and Crafts style. A guest at Russell House described the garden and its revivalist flavor in the poem "A Country House."

> An old world garden at the side is found
> Where saxifrage and roving woodruff run.
> Sweet William flashes rainbow patterns round
> And clove pinks toss their perfume to the sun.
> Here vagrant poppies flaunt their crumpled skirts
> And lift their brazen cheeks for bees to kiss.
> The golden lily with the lupine flirts

ALFRED PARSONS. *China Roses, Broadway*, c. 1900.
Watercolor on paper. Private collection, courtesy
Christopher Wood

With the addition of Russell House and Abbot's
Grange, the Millet garden expanded considerably,
as did Lily Millet's talents as a gardener. Here China
roses, Solomon's seal, and pansies line a grass path.

And frets her steeple blooms for higher bliss....
Great staring sunflowers face the traveling sun
And boldly strive to dim his yellow rays;
Whilst snow white stocks, as pure as any nun
Shrink from the gaudy pansies' eager gaze.
Tall dahlias spread their trains of varied hue
O'er humming carpets of sweet mignonette;
Phlox and verbena sip the lingering dew,
The fuchsia shakes her crimson epaulette.
But over all there hangs a glorious cloud
Of blooming roses, pink and white and red,
In such profusion that the plucked are proud
When cloying fingers tear them from their bed....
Across a dewy mead a pathway trips
To mullioned grange once filled with friars gay.
But still a flavour of the good old times
Lingers round the walls of his domain
And many a guest shall dream that Merrie England's back again.[34]

Garden house at Abbot's Grange, 1910.
Country Life Picture Library, London

In 1910, when Broadway had become a tourist destination and the residence of such celebrities as American actress Mary Anderson de Navarro, *Country Life* published an article on "Abbot's Grange and Russell House." By that date, the garden occupied the large triangular area between the houses and was laid out in grass paths with herbaceous borders. An arcade of rambler roses covered the walk to tennis and croquet lawns, and the central path led to a semicircular loggia made of columns rescued from an ancient building. Lily Millet now hybridized carnations with the help of Alfred Parsons, who had added to the garden tree peonies brought back from a trip to Japan.[35]

A few American artists settled elsewhere in England. Anna Lea, who was from a prominent Philadelphia Quaker family, determined to become a painter after seeing English Pre-Raphaelite William Holman Hunt's *Light of the World* in 1857. After the Civil War, her entire family traveled to Europe for an extended stay. In Florence she received her first instruction from a professor at the Academy of Fine Arts, to which women were not admitted. (During the same years, Anna Lea's contemporary Mary Cassatt, also from Philadelphia, sought private tutelage in France.) The Lea family was in Paris at the beginning of the Franco-Prussian conflict and managed to escape to London. When they returned to America in 1871, however, Anna stayed behind. She had begun to exhibit at the Royal Academy, and she rented a studio in the same building as the painting restorer Henry Merritt. She became his student and married him just a few months before his death in 1877.[36]

Anna Merritt then moved to Cheyne Walk in Chelsea. Whistler was a neighbor, and her idol Holman Hunt and other prominent English painters became friends. She gained renown for her portraits and allegorical subjects, such as *Love Locked Out* (1889), which depicts a nude boy seen from behind seeking admittance to a closed doorway covered in climbing roses, as his torch lies extinguished and his arrow broken on the doorstep. (She had made the original drawing in 1877 as a memorial to her husband, the doorway being that of a tomb.) In 1889 she also painted a portrait of Henry James and wrote, "With dear Henry James (everyone said "dear" Henry James) I quickly grew into a friendship." Until 1890, when debilitating illness struck, she enjoyed considerable financial and critical success.[37]

Clockwise from top left: ANNA LEA MERRITT, *Roses Midsummer*; *Iris, Pansies, and Foxglove*; *Anemone and Narcissus*; *Iceland and Shirley Poppies.* From Anna Lea Merritt, *An Artist's Garden*, 1908

Merritt's garden was in the village of Hurstbourne-Tarrant, on the Hampshire Downs.

In 1891 Anna Merritt left London in despair, rented a small cottage, The Limes, in a village on the Hampshire Downs, and made a garden that, she revealed, "became the great resource of my lonely life and old age." As she wrote in her charming account of the village: "The care of my flowers became a passion. Their wants and needs I studied as though they were conscious beings, as indeed I believe them to be."[38] Here she began a second career as a painter of landscapes and gardens, especially her own. Watercolors of the garden, reproduced in her book *An Artist's Garden* (1908), although freely painted in brilliant colors, remain realistic. She wrote: "I have not acquired the latest impressionist style, which so ably represents things as seen from a motor-car at full speed."[39]

Anna Merritt's garden mentor was Mrs. Wickham Flower, who had been a Chelsea neighbor in a house furnished and decorated by Morris and Company. In 1885 Mr. Flower bought Great Tangley Manor, a fifteenth-century half-timbered house in Surrey, and employed Arts and Crafts architect Philip Webb to advise on restoration. *Country Life* devoted three articles to the manor gardens, noting that no plan was drawn or written instructions given, which left open the question of ultimate responsibility for the design. The garden combined the formal and informal: a courtyard with herbaceous borders and enclosing walls covered in jasmine, wisteria, and guelder roses, a revivalist Tudor garden, and a bog garden with naturalized planting. Yew hedges separated lawn and meadow.[40]

Anna Merritt credited Mrs. Flower for "my first lessons in garden lore and work" and respected her "great experience in gardening."[41] Mrs. Flower's gifts of many plants and shrubs were the beginning of Merritt's garden. Her cottage was sheltered from the road by pollard lime trees and flowerbeds with box edging. A grass path between a border of berberis and pillar roses led to the lawn behind the cottage through an archway covered in clematis and roses. Beside the clipped yews marking the far boundary, she built a painting studio covered in climbing roses, and on the bank under the yews, she planted English woodland natives: primroses, violets, bluebells, Solomon's seal, woodruff, forget-me-nots, harebell, and wild orchids, together with plants that reminded her of home: trillium, gentians, dogtooth violets, and pansies.[42] She noted with pleasure that her cottage was not unlike her family's eighteenth-century home near Philadelphia, where the old-time garden also had clipped hedges with box edges for the beds.

For planting her borders, Anna Merritt studied Robinson's *The English Flower Garden* (1883) but trusted her artist's eye for arrangement. She felt that a garden "should be considered as a living picture and designed as carefully as a painting" by paying attention to form, light and shade, and contrasts and harmonies of color as does a painter. She arranged her flowers in "large effective groups of one color in varying shades in different heights and forms."[43] A hot border had crimson poppies and parrot tulips in spring and helianthus, rudbeckia, gaillardia, and nasturtiums in autumn. A delphinium bed was backed by *Clematis jackmanii* on a wall and bordered with *Veronica incana*. She considered annuals a snare for the unwary but admitted a fondness for fragrant ones such as mignonette and nicotiana. She felt poppies to be indispensable and combined orange and yellow Iceland poppies and Shirley poppies with iris. Small Irish yews marked the corners of the beds. Open areas of lawn offered contrast with intensively planted areas such as her rock garden, which was filled to overflowing with alpine pinks and phlox, geums, poppies, silenes, gentians, fritillaries, auriculas, saxifrages, thymes, aquilegia, and other tiny treasures, with great clumps of Madonna lilies nearby.

The most brilliant artist's garden in England, and the one with the most lasting influence, was that begun by Lawrence Johnston and his mother, Gertrude Waterbury Winthrop, at Hidcote Manor in Gloucestershire in 1907. Lawrence's father, Elliot Johnston, a Baltimore banker, had married Gertrude Waterbury, the daughter of a wealthy New York manufacturer, in 1870, and the couple left immediately for Europe. Lawrence Johnston was born in Paris, his brother in Switzerland, and his sister in Nice. After the death of the youngest child in 1874, the family returned to New York. Here Johnston's brother died, followed by his father

Old garden borders looking toward the circle and cedar lawn, c. 1910.
National Trust Photographic Library, London

Top: Pool garden from the circle at Hidcote, c. 1910.
National Trust Photographic Library, London

in 1884.[44] Three years later, Gertrude Johnston married New York lawyer Charles Frances Winthrop in London, where they resided for part of each year. Young Lawrence Johnston prepared for entrance to Trinity College, Cambridge, and was graduated in 1897. His stepfather died the next year, leaving Gertrude Winthrop to his care. In fact it proved to be the reverse, as Mrs. Winthrop held firmly onto both Johnston and the purse strings.[45]

In 1900 Lawrence became a naturalized British citizen and enlisted in the British Army, which was then fighting the Boer War in South Africa. He would remain in the army for twenty years, serving with distinction in World War I and retiring with the rank of major.[46] In the meantime, in 1907, his mother, perhaps tired of a trans-Atlantic life, bought at auction the 280-acre estate of Hidcote Bartrim in the Cotswolds. She seems to have hoped that her son would interest himself in the management of the farm during his leaves, while she gardened. The purchase, in any event, established Lawrence Johnston as an English gentleman, the heir to a country property in a fashionable region favored by designers and patrons of the Arts and Crafts Movement.

Neither Lawrence nor his mother had any formal architectural or horticultural training. Mrs. Winthrop had grown up on a country place in Westchester County, New York, and would have known estates there and in New England. She had many opportunities to view gardens in France and England with her son, who was developing a keen aesthetic sense.[47] There was no garden to speak of at Hidcote, but by the house within the old brick garden walls stood a magnificent cedar of Lebanon. This became the focus of the first garden area, the Cedar Lawn terrace enclosed in clipped hedges. The glorious spine of the garden—the long vista west from the cedar to the distant hills—may have been envisioned from the beginning. The garden enclosures within the old wall were the first to be completed, however, and were the least innovative. Mrs. Winthrop was initially the gardener; perhaps her taste prevailed here.

An opening in the south hedge of the Cedar Lawn led into the Phlox Garden (now the White Garden), a foursquare arrangement of box-bordered beds centered on a grass circle ornamented with a sundial. Similar old-fashioned gardens had been made since the 1870s throughout New England as well as in England; phlox was a New England favorite.[48] The area called the Old Garden, to the west of the Phlox Garden, was divided into four parallel beds planted with long-cultivated perennials in soft colors. These first garden areas have undergone changes over the intervening century, but the bones of Johnston's subsequent designs remain.

Lawrence Johnston's genius became evident as soon as the garden broke out of the old walls. A gate in the west wall of the Old Garden opens into a grass enclosure, the Circle, which offers a cross axis with stairs leading to enclosed circular beds, a round bathing pool at the lowest level, and a further grass roundel at the boundary of the garden. From the beginning he must have envisioned these as the brilliant architectural spaces they have become with the maturing of the enclosing tapestry hedges and topiary figures. More prescient is the use of the Circle as the transition to the bold Scarlet Borders, which draw the eye toward twin brick pavilions on a higher level and beyond to the *pallisade à l'italienne* of clipped hornbeam planted in 1915. This visually breathtaking progression upward past more hedge-enclosed plantings leads to airy iron gates, which allows a satisfying view of the valley and hills beyond.[49] The sprightly pagoda roofs of the twin pavilions offer amusing exclamation marks.

On his retirement from the army in 1920, Lawrence Johnston devoted himself to the garden and developed his horticultural knowledge through travel, his friendships with fellow gardeners, reading, and experimentation. The size of the garden expanded exponentially, beginning with the majestic Theater Lawn, then the Pillar Garden, stream garden, woodland, and more, pulled together by the cross axis of the dramatic Long Walk enclosed in hornbeam hedges.[50] His garden rooms offered a variety of sheltered microclimates for his treasures, many of which still flourish. For example, Mrs. Winthrop's garden, laid out in 1915 to the south of the Scarlet Borders, was a sun trap; plantings were intended to recall those of the Riviera, where both Johnston and his mother died.[51]

Like all great gardens, Hidcote grew organically in intimate response to place and time, informed by Lawrence Johnston's considerable talents and knowledge. His American background and lack of training in design were an advantage. Since he had few preconceived notions of what a garden should be, he was open to the best from both past and present. His painter's eye and keenly developed sense of architectural space and proportion resulted in a garden that was immensely satisfying and original, both aesthetically and botanically. Johnston's American friend in nearby Broadway, Mary Anderson de Navarro, wrote, "My Italian friends regard Hidcote as the most beautiful garden they have seen in England. Its wonderful blending of colors and its somewhat formal architectural character please them particularly."[52] In 1949, soon after Lawrence gave Hidcote to the National Trust, Vita Sackville-West visited and was impressed by the luxuriance of planting with "flowering shrubs mixed with Roses, herbaceous plants with bulbous subjects, climbers scrambling over hedges," a planting method she attributed to him.[53] ❧

Italian Garden at I Tatti, before 1926. Florence
Berenson Archive, reproduced by permission
of the President and Fellows of Harvard College

PUBLIC DISPLAYS AND PRIVATE WORLDS

Chapter Four

The marriage of beautiful Jennie Jerome, the daughter of Wall Street magnate Leonard Jerome, to Lord Randolph Churchill in 1874 began the entry en masse of American heiresses into the European marriage market. The burgeoning of new millionaires in the industrial expansion after the Civil War, and the desire of most to establish social credentials through marriage, resulted in hundreds of contenders for titles. By 1910 it was estimated that more than five hundred American women had married titled Europeans.[1]

A notice appeared in the London *Daily Telegraph* in 1902 advising that "[a]n English peer of very old title is desirous of marrying at once a very wealthy lady: her age and looks are immaterial, but her character must be irreproachable.... If among your clients you know such a lady, who is willing to purchase the rank of peeress for twenty-five thousand pounds sterling, paid in cash to her future husband, and who has sufficient wealth besides to keep up the rank of a peeress, I shall be pleased if you will communicate with me." This brutally frank advertisement was placed by the septuagenarian marquess of Donegall, who, after weathering several bankruptcies and wives, had chosen to set himself up again through matrimony. He found a taker in twenty-two-year-old Violet Twining, a graduate of Wellesley College, who reportedly agreed to support the marquess with an allowance of $40,000 a year. Ten months after the marriage, a son was born, who at just seven months of age succeeded his father as the sixth marquess.[2]

Violet's marriage was brief, and it left her with an heir to the title and the balance of her fortune intact. Many of the thousands of marriages made by American women to Europeans in the decades around 1900 did not end so happily. An Englishwoman writing about American brides pointed out that, as in political and cultural life, society remained the domain of the English male with the corollary "tacit understanding that the wife is the property of the husband." She added that "this elimination of personal independence and acceptance as part of the family has sometimes proved rather galling to proud, spirited American women."[3] Many novelists of the period treat this theme, few with the depth and nuance of Henry James. A typical example is *American Wives and English Husbands* (1898) by California writer Gertrude Atherton. Cecil Maundrell, the heir of Lord Barnstaple and hero of this melodrama, discloses the expectations of an English husband of his wife while proposing to his American bride: "She will obey him, she will have as many children as he wishes, her scheme of life will be his, and, no matter how bright she may be, she will adapt herself to him."[4]

As was often pointed out, the English aristocracy paid no attention to American class distinctions—all that mattered was wealth. Paradoxically, English society was now more open to wealthy Americans than was their own, and new money was as acceptable as old. In Atherton's novel, Cecil's bride complains of the Chicago-bred second wife of Lord Barnstaple: "It is rather odd having to stand just behind a stepmother whom I shouldn't think of knowing at home." Cecil explains that "of course there are no distinctions in regard to Americans over here; it is all personality and money."[5]

In many of these marriages for money and position, a demanding social life and the creation or restoration of houses and gardens temporarily distracted the partners from the paucity of their emotional rapport. Helena Zimmerman, the daughter of Cincinnati railroad and oil tycoon Eugene Zimmerman, married Kim, the ninth duke of Manchester, in 1900. (His father, the eighth duke, had also married an American heiress, Consuelo Iznaga from Louisana.) Mr. Zimmerman paid the duke's debts, settled an income on the couple, and gave them as a wedding present Kylemore Castle in County Galway, Ireland, built in the late 1860s. The property included nine thousand acres of moorland, a six-acre walled garden, and twenty-one greenhouses. In anticipation of a visit by King Edward VII and Queen Alexandra, the young couple reportedly spent $150,000 refurbishing the house and garden. (The king and queen stayed only for tea and never saw the garden.) Helena's marriage ended in divorce in 1931.[6]

An expected visit by the king and queen in 1907 spurred another American heiress, May

Goelet, duchess of Roxburghe, to invest $625,000 in the modernization of Floors Castle, the largest inhabited castle in Scotland, and in the complete reworking of its gardens.[7] May, the daughter of Ogden Goelet and May Wilson of New York, had grown up between New York and the French Riviera and had married Henry John, the eighth duke of Roxburghe, in 1903. The refurbished garden was significant enough to merit an article in *Country Life*, where the twelve-foot-wide borders in the walled garden were singled out for their "barbaric splendor and generosity of bloom." These box-edged borders flanked the wide central path and were backed with pillars and linking chains covered with climbing roses. Among the hardy flowers were American natives long used in English gardens: goldenrod, aster, black-eyed Susan, snakeroot, and phlox[8] (see illustration, page 6).

The happiest of marriages across the Atlantic, like those at home, were between relatively equal partners who had compatible temperaments and similar tastes. Occasionally, both had an interest in gardening. Joseph Chamberlain, a Birmingham manufacturer and Member of Parliament with a passion for orchids, arrived in Washington, D.C., in 1887, sent by the British government to negotiate a treaty on northern fisheries. Although he had already lost two wives, Joseph was a very attractive and youthful fifty-one. At a reception in the British Legation, he met beautiful twenty-three-year-old Mary Endicott of Salem, Massachusetts, and fell instantly in love. She was drawn to his intelligence and vitality, his passionate involvement in so much that was of interest to them both. He would write her: "Take my advice and never marry a politician, but you may marry a horticulturist—a grower of orchids, for instance."[9]

Mary Endicott's father, secretary of war under Grover Cleveland, was not happy about their engagement. Proud of his old family, he would have preferred an equally distinguished background for the

JOHN SINGER SARGENT.
Mary Endicott Chamberlain, 1902.
Oil on canvas. National Gallery of Art, Washington, D.C.

Mary Endicott from Massachusetts married English industrialist and politician Joseph Chamberlain in 1888 and went to live at his estate, Highbury, outside Birmingham.

Highbury from the southeast. *Gardeners' Chronicle*, 1904.
Royal Horticultural Society, Lindley Library, London

The pleasure grounds of Highbury, which were laid out in 1879, by 1900 occupied more than one hundred acres and included Mary Chamberlain's rose garden.

Top: A portion of the new grounds at Highbury. *Gardeners' Chronicle*, 1905.
Royal Horticultural Society, Lindley Library, London

In 1902 a two-acre meadow was planted with flowering trees and shrubs in meandering beds filled with perennials.

husband of his daughter. Nonetheless, Joseph Chamberlain overcame his opposition and married Mary at the end of the following year. She proved invaluable in his political career. As his biographer wrote, "Coming as she did from the aristocracy of the new world, Mary helped him make his way among the aristocracy of the old.... She counteracted the feeling that Joe was not quite a gentleman." In fact, he was the first industrialist to reach the highest rung in British politics.[10]

While courting Mary Endicott, Joseph Chamberlain's interests turned to roses, as they were her passion. He built a rose house for her at Highbury, his estate outside Birmingham, and in his letters he assured her that they would cultivate all her American favorites to remind her of home. He revealed that despite his financial and political success, "I have been so lonely, there has never been a time when I would not have accepted a sentence of death as a relief.... You have made life once more a glorious and a hopeful thing."[11]

Once settled at Highbury, the Chamberlains worked together creating fashionable Dutch and Italian gardens, building greenhouses, planting trees and shrubs, and making a suitable wild setting for the lake and stream crossed by rustic bridges. When in London for the sitting of Parliament, the Chamberlains frequented the Royal Botanic Gardens at Kew. During infrequent separations, they kept each other up to date on happenings in the garden and greenhouses, and at home they enjoyed tea among the roses and moonlight walks through the succession of gardens.

A visitor in 1896 noted that "Roses and Violets are among the favorite flowers of Mrs. Chamberlain," with roses appearing throughout the garden, as well as in the hedge-enclosed rosary. The borders were planted with large, irregular masses of hardy flowers, such as asters, lupins, pyrethrums, centaureas, campanulas, delphiniums, and hollyhocks among the shrubs. American natives such as *Cypripedium spectabile* (ladyslipper) and grasses lined the stream.[12]

It was more difficult for a wealthy American to be accepted as marriage material by the French aristocracy than by the English. As the author of the 1895 book *About Paris* pointed out, "The American princess cannot expect people who have had title and ancestors so long as to have forgotten them to look upon Sallie Sprigs of California as anything better than an Indian squaw."[13] Nonetheless, two daughters of Isaac Merritt Singer, the inventor of the first practical sewing machine, managed to marry three French princes. Having fathered eighteen children with four women, Isaac Singer fled in 1860 to Europe, where he began a legitimate family with his French second wife, the mother of his daughters Winnaretta and Isabelle. In 1867, after the birth of a son in Paris, he bought an estate in England near Torquay and built a mansion, The Wigwam, complete with a private theater, conservatories, and a garden in the latest style, with carpet beds and exotic trees. His attempt to enter good society by giving a grand ball was a failure, as none of the local gentry would attend.[14] Sadly, he did not live long enough to witness the triumphs of his daughters in the marriage market.

In 1888, on the marriage of Isabelle Singer to Duc Jean Élie Decazes, the *Herald-Tribune* headlined: "She pays all the bills—he thinks himself cheap at the price." A French journalist added: "It is evident already that French noblemen, properly married, decorated, appointed, housed and fed are very costly commodities for American heiresses to deal in."[15] Isabelle enjoyed her title for only eight years, for she died in 1896. The marriage of her elder sister, Winnaretta, to her first prince ended in divorce, and in 1893 she married Prince Edmond de Polignac, an amateur composer. After his death, Winnaretta came into her own as a noted hostess and patron of music, commissioning works from Stravinsky, Satie, and Poulenc, among others, for performance in her Paris salon.[16]

Several American heiresses chose to live abroad without considering marriage at all. At the turn of the century, France offered a degree of freedom to an unmarried woman not possible at home. Natalie Barney, from Washington, D.C., had attended boarding school in France for two years while her mother, Alice Pike Barney, studied painting with academician Charles Carolus-Duran. In 1898 Natalie returned to Paris with her mother, who enrolled in Whistler's

Académie Rossi. A blonde beauty, self-assured, highly intelligent, and athletic (she was known as L'Amazone), Natalie Barney was expected to marry well. Her intentions were otherwise, however, although she was briefly engaged to Mary Cassatt's nephew. In 1899 she initiated a stormy liaison with the celebrated courtesan Liane de Pougy, among the most newsworthy conquests in her long career as seductress. (Liane's fictionalized account of the affair, *Idylle sapphique*, was reprinted seventy times in 1901, the year it was published.[17]) At the same time, Barney established herself as a poet with her *Quelques portraits-sonnets de femmes* (1900).

The death of her father in 1903 left her independently wealthy and free to live as she wished. At her house in Neuilly, Barney entertained writers, artists, musicians, and other cultural notables at dinners and theatrical events. In 1908 she found a permanent home in a two-story seventeenth-century *pavillon* at 20, rue Jacob. The garden had the remnants of a forest, including an ancient towering chestnut, and at the back, a four-column Doric temple inscribed under the pediment "À L'Amitié." The Temple to Friendship became the focus of Barney's fêtes in the garden and of her Friday salons, which attracted international literary and artistic notables.[18] Painter Romaine Brooks, who moved to Paris in 1905, was one of these—and Barney's affair with her endured for fifty years.

Not every unattached aristocrat chose to marry money. Quite a few preferred to make it for themselves. One young Scotsman, Robert Burnett, eldest son of the third son of Sir Robert Burnett, laird of Crathes Castle in Banchory, Scotland, had no expectation of inheriting and set out for America to seek his fortune. Upon arriving in Los Angeles in 1859, Burnett promptly sent home seeds of the impressive Wellingtonias and Douglas firs he found there, the origin of the present conifer glade to the west of Crathes Castle.[19] The following year, he bought a ranch and 24,000 head of sheep. Comfortably established, in 1864 he married Matilda, the daughter of James and Mary Murphy of New York and a well-to-do divorcée. By 1872 Burnett had acquired title to more than 25,000 acres in Los Angeles. When he

ROMAINE BROOKS. *Natalie Barney, "L'Amazone."* 1920.
Oil on canvas. Musée Carnavalet, Paris

View of the gardens from
the southwest, Crathes Castle,
Banchory, Scotland, 1893.
The Studio, 1897

This drawing shows the
upper gardens and the lower
walled *potager* as they were
when Sir Robert Burnett,
the eleventh laird, lived there
with his American wife,
Matilda Murphy. Sir Robert
had made a fortune as a rancher
in California and restored
the gardens.

inherited Crathes in 1876, following the successive deaths of his two uncles and father, he had
a small fortune to spend on enhancing the eighteenth-century garden there.[20]

Walls enclosed nearly four acres of garden to the east of the castle. The centerpiece of the
upper garden was a double file of yew topiaries, dating from about 1702, which divided the
space into four unequal sections. They had been engulfed in later yew hedges; only their tops
were evident. The lower vegetable garden was also divided into quadrants, which centered on
an ancient Portugal laurel clipped into an umbrella. The Burnetts' decision to keep the garden
intact—adding a rose garden within one upper quadrant and wide borders filled with masses of
traditional perennials in the lower garden—was in keeping with revivalist sentiment. Such
gardens were newly fashionable in both Britain and America.

The reputation of the garden spread, and in 1893 architect J. J. Joass came to make a meas-
ured drawing for his article on formal gardens in Scotland.[21] In 1895 Gertrude Jekyll visited with
watercolorist Samuel Elgood. She recorded that "the finest of the hardy flowers are well grown
in bold groups" and noted luxuriant phlox, tansy, pyrethrum, rudbeckia, *Maclea cordata*,
Japanese anemones, and climbing roses. She attributed to the Scottish climate and long hours
of daylight in summer the "brilliancy of the colour masses" in the generous borders.[22] Their
floral splendor was documented in two watercolors included in *Some English Gardens* (1903).[23]

A year after Sir Robert Burnett inherited Crathes, the famous feminist Victoria Woodhull and her sister, Tennessee Claflin, traveled to England, bankrolled by William H. Vanderbilt. His position as heir to the estate of his father Commodore Cornelius Vanderbilt was being contested in court by his siblings, and Victoria had letters from the commodore that would compromise William Vanderbilt's case. Her payoff for relinquishing them was a fresh start in London in

1877, where she continued her lectures on spiritualism. At one lecture, entitled "The Garden of Eden," she was noticed by banker John Biddulph Martin, who promptly fell in love with her but could not convince his family of her respectability. Like Nancy Headway, the self-promoting heroine of Henry James's story "The Siege of London" (1882), Victoria Woodhull made valiant attempts to bury her disreputable past as a publicity-seeking charlatan in order to gain acceptance into an upper-class family. She was married to Martin in 1882, but she continued to be shunned by polite society.[24] After her husband's death in 1897, she was more successful in making a place for herself at the Martin country estate, Bredon's Norton, on the river Avon near Tewksbury. Here she took up gardening and established a local flower show, where her efforts were rewarded by a visit from the Prince of Wales.

GEORGE SAMUEL ELGOOD.
Above: Double Herbaceous Borders at Crathes Castle, 1895; *right: Yew Topiary at Crathes Castle*, 1895. From George Samuel Elgood and Gertrude Jekyll, *Some English Gardens*, 1904.

Victoria's sister, Tennie, had an easier time adapting to life abroad. In London she met a wealthy widower, Sir Francis Cook, and convinced him that his dead wife's spirit wanted them to marry. He did not need much convincing, as Tennie was both charming and light-hearted, and they were married in 1885. As Lady Cook, viscountess of Montserrat in Portugal, Tennie presided over a significant garden filled with rarities that was open to the public.[25]

A young woman from a distinguished family in Geneseo, New York, Cornelia Wadsworth Ritchie, had a difficult time with the notoriety of John George Adair (known as Black John), the Irishman she married in 1867. He had made a fortune

Glenveigh Castle. *1888* Co. Donegal.

by buying up bankrupt farms during the Famine and, in 1861, had evicted all of the tenants on his 22,000-acre estate, Glenveagh in County Donegal, the last major eviction in Ireland. Most families had nowhere to go but the workhouse or Australia.[26]

After clearing the land and marrying Cornelia Ritchie, who was then a wealthy widow, John Adair commissioned a baronial castle for the most scenic position on Lough Veagh. Building was complete in 1873, the Adairs settled in, and Cornelia began to improve the stark and treeless surroundings. Masses of Austrian and Scots pine and *Rhododendron ponticum* were planted, a vegetable garden laid out, and in a sheltered position to the east of the castle, the two-acre pleasure ground was begun. This required massive moving of earth to level the thin,

Above: Postcard of Glenveagh Castle, County Donegal, Republic of Ireland, 1888. Glenveagh Archives

Cornelia Ritchie, a wealthy American widow, married Irish landowner John Adair in 1867 and they built Glenveagh Castle on his estate at Lough Veagh.

Cornelia Ritchie Adair and her dog Patty at Glenveagh Castle. Glenveagh Archives

After her husband's death in 1885, Cornelia developed the pleasure grounds of the estate.

boggy soil and to provide planting space for more rhododendrons, native oaks, and Japanese maples around a lawn.[27]

The atmosphere in Donegal must have been increasingly unpleasant for the Adairs, as they left for America in 1875. After selling some inherited land in Geneseo, New York, they headed west, eventually settling in Texas, where they owned or leased nearly a million acres for cattle on the Texas panhandle, still known as the J. A. Ranch. This was clearly territory more congenial to John Adair's character and ruthless business methods.

His death there in 1885 left his widow free to return to Glenveagh, where she was to spend most autumns until World War I. Her warm nature and charitable work in the community made her as welcome as her husband had been shunned. She hosted convivial shooting and fishing parties for her English and American friends, but her focus remained the garden, which she continued to improve. She planted more rhododendrons and other shrubs around the pleasure ground and had drives made to high points on the hill behind the castle for spectacular views of the grounds and lake. The mature trees and shrubs made the grounds of Glenveagh a green and lovely oasis in the stark landscape. As a departing guest in 1893 wrote to Cornelia Adair, "you and nature both combine/To form a paradise on earth/And make Glenveagh to all divine."[28]

The English landscape architect Harold A. Peto arrived for a weekend in August 1905 to have a look.[29] He found there grounds more sympathetic to Frederick Law Olmsted or William Robinson than to the Renaissance-inspired formal gardens then being espoused by architects J. D. Sedding (*Garden Craft Old and New*, 1891) and Sir Reginald Blomfield (*The Formal Garden in England*, 1892). At Cornelia Adair's Glenveagh there were no clipped hedges, geometric arrangement of plants, or axial vistas.

Cornelia Adair's grandson sold Glenveagh in 1929 to another American, Harvard professor Arthur Kingsley Porter, whose restoration work on the property ceased when he disappeared mysteriously off the coast of Donegal four years later.[30] In 1937, Henry P. McIlhenny, curator of decorative arts at the Philadelphia Museum of Art, bought Glenveagh from Porter's widow. His grandfather had grown up nearby before his emigration to America, where his father had amassed a fortune through his invention of the gas meter. Young Henry McIlhenny, who was renowned for his fine collection of nineteenth-century paintings and furniture, brought his trained eye and cultivated taste to bear on both castle and garden.

McIlhenny stated that he became a serious gardener only after his return from service in

MORTON KAISH. *The Garden at Glenveagh*, 1979. Oil on canvas. Smithsonian Institution American Art Museum, Washington, D.C.

Henry P. McIlhenny, from Philadelphia, bought Glenveagh in 1937. He made a plantsman's paradise of the pleasure grounds and developed the *potager* as the brilliant display of colorful vegetables and flowers seen in this painting.

the Navy in World War II. Beginning in the 1950s, English nurseryman James Russell gave advice and supplied plants, and the landscape designer Laning Roper, McIlhenny's Harvard classmate, was frequently consulted as well.[31] Nonetheless, the garden is evidence of Henry's own particular tastes and enthusiasms. He added a collection of large-leafed rhododendrons and tree ferns to the mature trees of Cornelia Adair's pleasure ground. He often said he could not abide bare ground and adored large-leafed plants, hence hosta, rogersia, bergenia, phormium, and occasionally gunnera provide transitions to the large, irregular lawn. Candelabra primulas, Himalayan poppies, astilbes, and agapanthus nestle alongside. The large scale of these understory plants and the exciting contrasts of leaf size and texture create a manicured jungle.

Cordelia Adair's path through the wood above the pleasure ground was enhanced with clearings along its length. For one of these, Roper suggested a formal terrace decorated with antique sculpture and terra-cotta pots. As McIlhenny wrote, "One can get tired of endless naturalistic plantings, and long for formality, straight lines and hedges."[32] A vista was cut connecting the pleasure ground with the kitchen garden and new garden areas. A particularly attractive aspen in the path did not bother him—it still stands in the middle of the view. The new axis culminated in the semicircular hedges of the view garden that frame Lough Veagh.

In the kitchen garden, now a *potager* with its new enclosing stone wall, Henry McIlhenny indulged his taste for brilliant color and contrasts of shape. He delighted in creating scores of flower arrangements for the castle, so the walls and the central walk were flanked with wide borders filled with masses of annuals and perennials for cutting as well as effect. White flowers and white-variegated foliage were particular favorites, and lilies were his special passion. One vista was lined with what he called "an almost vulgar display" of *Lilium auratum*. Letters from Roper to the Glenveagh estate manager reveal another obsession with giant lily, *Cardocrinum giganteum*.[33]

McIlhenny wrote that he preferred to plant for effect rather than to show off botanical rarities, but he achieved both aims. The gardens at Glenveagh, which he gave to the Republic of Ireland in 1983, offer formal vistas, naturalistic exuberance, and a wealth of exotic, frost-tender plants, rare rhododendrons, and majestic trees in a starkly beautiful setting.

In 1885, the same year that Cornelia Adair returned from Texas to Glenveagh and its gardens, William Waldorf Astor ended a three-year stay in Rome as American minister to Italy. The grandson of John Jacob Astor, William had started in politics in New York as a state assemblyman and senator but was defeated in a run for Congress after a particularly acrimonious campaign.[34] Disgusted with American politics and the press, he found that his stay in Italy had whetted his appetite for the aesthetic riches of Europe. The death of his father in 1890 freed him to leave the United States permanently; he became a British subject in 1899. On his departure, he was quoted as exclaiming "America is not a fit place for a gentleman to live."[35]

Endowed with an active historical imagination (he had written two romances set in Renaissance Italy) and a sizeable fortune, William Astor was able to create spectacular settings for his vision of himself as the inheritor of baronial privilege. His first purchase was the Italianate mansion Cliveden, near London, from the duke of Westminister. Here Astor installed some of the booty he had brought from Italy—most prominently from the Borghese garden, a two-hundred-foot-long balustrade that was used to line the terrace at Cliveden. To protect himself from intruders, Astor erected a high wall topped with broken glass around the property, prompting the taunt "Waldorf by name and walled off by nature."[36] When he presented Cliveden to his oldest son, on the occasion of his marriage to Virginia beauty Nancy Langhorne in 1906, William had found his ideal residence.

William Astor's passion was for the Middle Ages, as well as for antiquity. He ran his various enterprises from Astor House, a medieval revival office building, and in 1903 bought Hever Castle, a thirteenth-century moated manor associated with Anne Boleyn. The reconstruction of the buildings and the making of a garden out of overgrown marshes and meadow in order to reflect his vision, took five years and reportedly ten million dollars. Astor had an entire medieval-style village constructed to house visitors and staff, and he hired a landscaping firm with hundreds of men to carry out his ideas for the garden. These included medieval revival topiary gardens near the castle, a thirty-five-acre lake, a rock garden and rhododendron walk, and a colossal four-acre Italian garden designed to showcase Astor's collection of antiquities.

In the Italian garden, he used a device he had tried on a small scale in the garden of his Villa Tritone at Sorrento—a high wall divided into niches designed to display a gallimaufry of sculpture, urns, well-heads, sarcophagi, amphorae, and broken columns. This monumental Pompeian Wall (one-eighth of a mile long and twelve feet high) on one side of the Italian garden was echoed by a pergola of equal length and height on the other. Along the wall, the numerous bays with their steps, recesses, and pergolas were screened with climbers and planted with flowering shrubs and perennials, including many Mediterranean varieties. The effect was of an ancient structure that had reverted to nature, suggestive of the romantic, vegetation-covered classical ruins that had fired Astor's imagination in Italy.[37]

This Italian garden is both an exercise in romantic nostalgia for the lost splendors of Rome and a reflection of Beaux-Arts design in its axial sequence of large, open spaces framed by classical structures.[38] At the entrance, a Roman triton was reflected in a semicircular pool and backed by a high yew hedge. A yew hedge divided the enormous rectangular space and within

ERNEST ARTHUR ROWE. *The Half-Moon Pond, Hever Castle*, 1920. Pencil and watercolor on paper. Collection Derrick Rowe

the larger division, a square enclosure contained a sunken garden with a Roman bath. The garden terminated in a gargantuan loggia flanked by colonnades that open onto a terrace and a lakeside piazza.

The baronial aspirations evident in Astor's garden at Hever Castle were at last gratified during World War I. His massive contributions to the British war effort earned him the longed-for title Baron Astor of Hever in 1916; he was the first native-born American to be ennobled. The following year he was named Viscount Astor, a hereditary title, at once spoiling his son Waldorf's political career as a Member of Parliament and launching that of Waldorf's American wife, Nancy Astor.

The year before Astor bought Hever Castle and began his garden, Rudyard Kipling and his American wife moved into an early-seventeenth-century house called Bateman's in Sussex. Caroline Balestier had grown up in Vermont and came to England with her

ERNEST ARTHUR ROWE
Top to bottom:
Hever Castle, 1920.
Pencil and watercolor on paper. Christie's Images, Ltd.

William Waldorf Astor bought Hever Castle, the home of Anne Boleyn, in 1903. This topiary bird stood in the Tudor revival garden beside the castle.

The Italian Garden, Hever Castle, 1920.
Pencil and watercolor on paper. Christie's Images, Ltd.

Astor had first used niches for the display of antique fragments in his garden at Sorrento when he was the American minister to Italy.

A Walkway Covered with the American Pillar Rose, Hever Castle, 1920.
Pencil and watercolor on paper. Christie's Images, Ltd.

brother, a popular literary agent. She wrote delightedly to her mother in 1890: "We have discovered that we can get Henry James when we really want him and so we are going to indulge him and let him stay away except when he is really needed to impress."[39] Rudyard Kipling became a friend, as well; indeed, Henry James served as best man at Kipling's precipitate wedding to Caroline, which followed the sudden death of her brother. The Kiplings lived for a time in Brattleboro, Vermont, but returned to England in 1896. They were delighted to find Bateman's, once an ironmonger's fine stone house, where Rudyard's imaginative stories found embodiment and Carrie could indulge her need to control every aspect of her husband's life.[40]

SIR EDWARD POYNTER. *Bateman's*, 1913.
Watercolor on paper. National Trust Photo Library, Angelo Hornak

It was here that Rudyard Kipling wrote "The Glory of the Garden," published in 1911. The last verse is familiar, with its exclamation, "And the Glory of the Garden it shall never pass away!"[41] Another verse suggests that both of the Kiplings were active gardeners:

> There's not a pair of legs so thin, there's not a head so thick
> There's not a hand so weak and white, nor yet a heart so sick
> But it can find some needful job that's crying to be done
> For the glory of the garden glorifieth every one.

The garden, located between the house and the stream, included terraced lawns, a clipped yew hedge on stilts, and a large square pool with a narrow channel leading to a circular pool in the rose garden laid out to Rudyard's design.[42]

A brilliant interpretation of an Italian Renaissance garden was created for an American couple resident in Italy, art historian Bernard Berenson and his wife. Berenson had been a protégé of Charles Eliot Norton at Harvard and met Isabella Stewart Gardner, who provided funds for his trip to Europe after graduation. He sent her in 1894 one of the first fruits of his study, his book *Venetian Painters of the Renaissance*. Isabella had begun to collect old masters. (She had recently bought at an auction, attended with Ralph Curtis, Vermeer's *Concert* for

Geoffrey Scott and Bernard Berenson in the Italian garden at I Tatti, 1915. Florence, Berenson Archive, reproduced by permission of the President and Fellows of Harvard College

Bernard and Mary Berenson bought I Tatti in 1907 and began restoration of the house and layout of the garden under the direction of Geoffrey Scott and Cecil Pinsent.

Top: Library Garden at I Tatti, 1915. Florence, Berenson Archive, reproduced by permission of the President and Fellows of Harvard College

$6,000.) Berenson became her advisor and over the next decade would handle a succession of masterpieces for her. At the same time, he became the leading agent for Italian Renaissance works of art in Europe.

In 1900 Bernard was finally able to marry recently widowed Philadelphia native Mary Costelloe, who had been both his lover and his collaborator in research, and they rented a farmhouse, I Tatti, at Settignano, outside Florence. Here they began to create a refuge for friends, students, and fellow scholars of Renaissance art, who were increasingly influenced by what Berenson had to say. For him, the deep knowledge and appreciation of art gave access to a realm that transcended ordinary life. As he explained, "the aesthetic moment is that flitting instant so brief as to be almost timeless, when the spectator is at one with the work of art he is looking at.... The two become one entity; time and space are abolished."[43] This spiritual dimension to the study of art, its life-enhancing quality, was enshrined at I Tatti, in both house and garden.

In 1907 the Berensons were able to buy I Tatti, and Mary invited Englishman Geoffrey Scott to advise them on remodeling. Scott's Oxford friend Cecil Pinsent was called in to design the grounds, which were well under way by 1910. This was the first commission for Scott and Pinsent and all did not go smoothly. Bernard Berenson wrote at the end of the year: "Outside it is too horrible. We have wasted a small fortune on the garden with the result of turning what was a dear Italian *podere* into a potter's field." As was his habit, Bernard went off on a trip, leaving Mary to deal with the difficulties.[44] The formal garden, inspired by those of the Renaissance, was laid out in terraces on the south of the house, the entire garden enclosed in cypress hedges. A box parterre, where flowers were permitted, was entered from the house. On the terrace below was the long building for over-wintering potted lemon trees. A double, curved stairway led from the central archway of this *limonaia* into the main garden beyond—a tiered sequence of clipped box rectangles punctuated with lemons in pots flanking the central path of pebble mosaic.

By 1912 the garden was coming together, and the evergreen oak woods beyond the garden had been planted. Through the cypress hedge beyond the twin pools at the bottom of the formal garden, a sculpture in a mosaic niche could be seen in the midst of the trees. Bernard, a perfectionist, had many suggestions for changes, but to the relief of Mary and Pinsent, left on another trip.[45] The cypress allée to the east of the formal garden was growing up, and the English meadow to the west was filled with species tulips, hellebore, grape hyacinths, daffodils, and anemones, as well as wildflowers. A new library addition had its own parterre garden. Mary supervised the garden and wrote Isabella Gardner: "I find the garden the greatest help and consolation in growing old."[46] Bernard, until the end of his life, enjoyed it each day he was in residence. He was an enthusiastic walker; a favorite route lay through the formal garden, out through the wood, up the cypress allée and along the various paths that meandered through the meadow.[47]

Pinsent was to design other formal Italian gardens for American and English expatriates. In 1915 Lady Sybil Cutting, widow of American William Bayard Cutting and amorously involved with Bernard Berenson, asked Pinsent to reconstruct the parterres on the lower terrace and east terrace of the historic Villa Medici at Fiesole. Lady Sybil's daughter, Iris Cutting, had been brought up in Italy according to her father's wishes that she "really be cosmopolitan deep down" and "be free to love and marry anyone she likes, of any country, without it being difficult."[48] She married Marchese Antonio Origo in 1924 and commissioned Pinsent to design a garden for their rural property, La Foce, in southern Tuscany.

At the Villa Medici as a child, Iris had preferred the evergreen oak wood and farmland to the box-edged beds and fountains. She had enjoyed, on her grandparents' Long Island estate, the collection of trees, shrubs, and ferns, the natural woodland and marsh, and the flowers.[49] Her first garden at La Foce was filled with roses. Flowers and climbers softened Pinsent's formal enclosures and lined the vital spine of the garden—a six-hundred-foot-long arbor that began at the house, overlooked Pinsent's garden rooms and a rose garden, and, following the contours of the hill, led to the family chapel and cemetery in a woodland. The Origo's seven-year-old son, Gianni, died of meningitis in 1933, and Pinsent designed for the new cemetery at

Marguerite Chapin, Bernard Berenson, and Rafreddo Caetani, 1912. Florence, Berenson Archive, reproduced by permission of the President and Fellows of Harvard College

Marguerite Chapin had married Prince Rafreddo Caetani in 1911 and would have a strong influence on the garden at Ninfa beginning in the 1930s.

the edge of the woods a simple temple as a chapel. Characteristically, Iris planted the cemetery with roses, something unheard-of in Italy.

Iris Origo had become an ardent plantswoman, aided by her friendship with American-born Contessa Mary Senni, who specialized in irises at Villa Senni near Rome. Iris visited her often, and in 1931 the two began a magazine *Il Giardino Fiorito* (The Flower Garden) aimed at amateurs who gardened on a small scale.[50]

Another American gardening friend and intellectual companion was Marguerite Chapin, who met young composer Prince Rafreddo Caetani when she was in Paris studying music. They married in 1911 and lived for twenty years at Versailles, where Marguerite edited an influential literary magazine. On the death of Rafreddo's brother Prince Gelasio, the Caetanis with their son, Camillo (who had inherited Gelasio's estate), and daughter, Lelia, went to live in Italy. Gelasio and his English mother had begun the clearing of the abandoned thirteenth-century town of Ninfa, twenty miles south of Rome, and the planting of trees and climbing roses among the ruins. Rafreddo and Marguerite continued the work and created an enchanting and romantic realm, unique among gardens. Rafreddo diverted a lake to run in myriad streams through the garden, while Marguerite concentrated on planting—more roses, wisteria, jasmine, and clematis over the walls, fruit trees for spring blossom, magnolias, viburnums and mimosa, and masses of perennials.[51]

After World War II, in which Camillo was killed, Marguerite founded a literary magazine with international contributors and circulation. The garden at Ninfa became a sanctum for writers, and Sunday lunch was always a special occasion. One recalled, "We never went indoors. Canvas chairs were scattered beneath trees along the river Ninfa.... Lunch was always preceded by a ritual tour of the garden, unless the visitor was severely infirm or sufficiently firm-minded to remain seated. First-time guests or favored friends were conducted either by Marguerite, or by the Caetani daughter, Lelia, who, like her mother, knew every leaf and blade of grass."[52]

This enchanted garden caught the imagination of author Georgio Bassani, who acknowledged that his novel *The Garden of the Finzi-Continis* (1962) had its origins there. He wrote: "Like the Finzi-Contini, the Caetani had taken refuge in a world of their own: cultured and refined, which protected them and at the same time excluded the rest of the world."[53]

A garden made on the Côte d'Azur at the end of World War I is a paradigm of this desire for a separate world. Henry Clews, Jr., after several unhappy years on Wall Street in his father's firm, determined to become an artist. Essentially self-taught, Clews had gone to Paris in 1901 with his first wife and painted full time. With his second wife, Elsie Ogden Goelet (whom Clews renamed Marie, as his sister was also Elsie), he returned to Paris and began to sculpt fantastic figures as well as portrait busts.[54] He lived through World War I in Paris, an experience that spurred

Above: Henry and Marie Clews, Mancha, Louise, nurse, and maid in the garden. Clews family archives

The Clews moved from Paris to La Napoule in 1919. Here Marie Clews found an outlet for her artistic talent in renovating the ancient château and planning a garden. She also delighted in designing fanciful costumes for her family and employees.

The Philosopher's Walk, Château La Napoule. Clews family archives

Henry Clews stands under the pergola in the Roman Garden on the right of the Allée of Honor.

his withdrawal into his imagination. He wrote: "The recent war gave some idea to what extent man has become degenerated by science and machinery.... I propose that we immediately begin to unmechanize, uninvent our way out of these scientific catacombs of unbelief, artificial pleasure, false happiness, machine idolatry and suffocating vulgarity into the sunlight of belief, full-hearted Elizabethan merriment, self-expression, vital refinement and true happiness."[55]

In 1919 Henry, Marie, and their young son, Mancha (Henry viewed himself as a latter-day Don Quixote), moved to Château La Napoule, a medieval fortress overlooking the sea near Cannes. They spent the next twenty years remaking the château and its Victorian grounds of pines, palms, eucalyptus, and cedars into the embodiment of a mystical realm that existed only in Henry's mind, an affirmation of their partnership. As his son wrote about Henry, "He had withdrawn from society in order to dedicate his life to the creation of art and to shape a lifestyle reflecting the glories of the past." In this Marie was the guiding spirit, despite her disclaimers in her memoir, aptly titled *Once Upon a Time at La Napoule*.[56]

Marie first had a studio made for Henry in a wing of the château. The Victorian chimneys were replaced with crenellated battlements; an arcaded cloister (the porphyry columns crowned with grotesque beasts sculpted by Henry) was built; and the interior was embellished with sculptural decoration. In the garden, a terrace supported by an arched wall was made along the waterfront. The remaining palms were extirpated, and a pergola, called the Philosopher's Walk, was built. The eucalyptus allée leading from the entrance to the courtyard of the château was replaced with clipped box and yew. On one side a Roman garden was created, its sunken basin reached by more sculptured columns. On the other side, what had been a tennis lawn was lined with sculptured sarcophagi, and a path beyond a hedge led to the arched wall. The remaining cypress made strong vertical accents within green spaces planted only with white flowers. White birds—ibis, cranes, white peacocks, and a marabou—enlivened the space. Even the two pet bulldogs were white. Three smaller areas were developed into the foursquare Venetian well garden, a guesthouse garden, and the mausoleum garden. The entire realm, encircled with formidable stone walls, was nearly invisible from the road, but from the sea it loomed like some mirage of medieval splendor.

After Henry Clew's death in 1937, Marie continued adding to the buildings and gardens. During World War II, she stayed on at the château to protect Henry's sculptures and to care for the garden. As the château was strategically located on the coast, the Germans installed gun emplacements in the courtyard. Always intrepid, Marie left to stay with a neighbor only when

The garden,
Château La
Napoule. Clews
family archives

the Allies were close—their first beachhead on the coast in 1944 included La Napoule. Luckily, there was little damage from bombardment. After the war, Marie covered the concrete gun emplacements with ivy and used them to store gardening tools. In 1950 she established La Napoule as an art foundation to exhibit Henry Clew's sculpture and to promote the appreciation of American art in France. At her death in 1959, she had the satisfaction of knowing that her own life's work, as well as Henry's sculptures, had been preserved and would be enjoyed by visitors in the future. ⌀

The Baroque quadrant in the Walled Garden at
Haseley Court. Andrew Lawson Photography

Chapter Five

Henry James, born in New York City in 1843, traveled back and forth to Europe as a young man but lived abroad permanently after 1875. His novels, short stories, articles, letters, and journals provide a unique window into the American expatriate communities in England, France, and Italy. He noted gardens abroad for their cultural associations and as social gathering spots, but evinced little interest in horticulture. Nonetheless, after acquiring his own house and garden in the Sussex seaside town of Rye in 1897, he was intrigued. He wrote despairingly: "I am *densely* ignorant—only just barely know dahlias from mignonette—and shall never be able to work it in any way."[1] Alfred Parsons, a noted gardener as well as a painter, arrived to give him encouragement. James reported to his sister that Parsons had "revealed to me the most charming possibilities for the tiny out-of-door part...an acre of garden and lawn, all shut in by the peaceful old red wall on which the most flourishing old espaliers, apricots, pears, plums and figs, assiduously grow."[2]

By the next year, Henry James was hooked. He had simplified the arrangement of beds and extended the lawn to the angle between the house and his writing room. He wrote his sister-in-law that he and his gardener had planted hundreds of hyacinths, tulips, and crocus, together with "innumerable unsightly roots and sprigs that I am instructed to depend upon as the fixed foundation of a future herbaceous and perennial paradise. Little by little, even with other cares, the slowly but surely working poison of the garden-mania begins to stir in my long-sluggish veins."[3] In mid-February, he noted happily that the crocus, hyacinths, primrose, and daffodils were blooming and the lawn was green. A neighbor advised planting nicotiana among the lupins. James did so and also ordered more than one hundred roses, his particular favorite, together with sweet peas, carnations, and fuchsias. In one year his flowers won thirteen prizes in a local show.

James was vastly proud of his modest garden and frequently mentioned it in letters to his family. He noted in August 1899 "the prettiest moment of the summer…the splendid bignonia throwing out its rich red flowers up and down the south wall, the big purple clematis flushing *à l'envis*, and the wisteria heavily, or rather lightly, draping the porch of my study."[4] He enjoyed showing his garden off to visitors, as well. American writer Sarah Orne Jewett and a friend came for lunch, which was served in the parlor overlooking the garden, and then took a stroll around the grounds. Edith Wharton was a frequent guest and recalled her visits with James in her autobiography, *A Backward Glance* (1934): "The arrival at Lamb House was almost a ritual performance…arm and arm we wandered out onto the thin worn turf of the garden, with its ancient mulberry tree, its unkempt flower-borders…the creeper-clad walls, and the scent of roses spiced with the strong smell of the sea."[5]

Wharton was in a position to notice "unkempt flower-borders," since she had created well-manicured ones at The Mount, her home in Lenox, Massachusetts. In 1904, when she and

James established their friendship, he visited The Mount and reported that the garden was "a monument to the almost too impeccable taste of its so accomplished mistress."[6] (It was in this year that Wharton's *Italian Villas and Their Gardens* was published.) Wharton had spent many years in Europe as a child and, once married, had traveled there annually. After selling The Mount, Wharton and her husband moved to Paris, where she remained after her divorce in 1913. She would make two magnificent gardens in France after World War I, but in the meantime her love of gardens was nurtured by her friendships and visits with the Bernard Berensons, the Ralph Curtises,

century furniture and objects for their rooms, the Gays furnished the garden with appropriate decorations, including a Clodion sculpture of dancing girls and a group of putti holding a dolphin, which was placed by the moat. In fine weather, guests were entertained for lunch or dinner on the terrace under the linden trees or were served tea in a small garden pavilion. In 1908 Bernard Berenson, who had just embarked on renovations at I Tatti, paid a visit and reported to his wife, "it is a dream of your and my kind of thing. Of course far grander than anything we can hope to attain."[10]

The Gays enjoyed visiting as well. A childhood friend of Matilda Gay's, Bessie Marbury, a leading New York theatrical agent, had just acquired Villa Trianon at Versailles in 1906, when the Gays drove over to attend a garden party. Matilda noted both the house, "most tastefully arranged by Elsie de Wolfe," and the garden, "also carefully laid out in the epoch, and everything is in the same note of harmony."[11] Elsie de Wolfe and Bessie Marbury had lived together in New York during de Wolfe's years as a professional actress. They were noted for their brilliant parties, which mixed artists, writers, actors, and society figures, a tradition that continued at Versailles.

In 1906 Elsie de Wolfe was just becoming known as a decorator as a result of her interiors for the new Colony Club in New York, where she had introduced pale colors, English chintz, and French furniture. At Versailles she restored Villa Trianon in the style of Louis XV. The color scheme of blue and

Top to bottom:
Tapis vert with box-bordered beds, garden of Elsie de Wolfe, Versailles

Square pool, garden of Elsie de Wolfe

Ivy arches and herbaceous border, garden of Elsie de Wolfe

From Reginald T. Townsend, ed., *The Book of Gardens and Gardening*, 1924 cream was based on that of the eighteenth-century boiserie acquired from an American friend living at Versailles, Minnie Paget, marchioness of Anglesey. The marchioness also introduced the pair into a lesbian society that included Winnaretta Singer, the princesse de Polignac.[12]

In her autobiography, de Wolfe described Villa Trianon as "the garden spot of my world." She had consulted the conservator of the Château de Versailles for advice on both house and garden, which adjoined the park of the château. The two salons and the dining room, which faced the garden, were given a terrace the length of the house. The grounds were divided into *potager*, greenhouse, and a pleasure garden that opened out from the terrace. A *tapis vert* with a central walkway ran from the terrace to a trellis-backed fountain. The walk was lined with beds of blue aubretia (echoing the color of the villa's interiors) and yews clipped into cones. More topiaries in the shape of horses, elephants, and birds were scattered about. A marble by Clodion of a nymph holding an infant faun stood on a lawn that was bordered with ivy planted on arches that framed rosebushes. An octagonal music pavilion of trelliswork served for receptions and provided changing rooms for the swimming pool. The enclosing privet hedge had an herbaceous border of delphiniums, Canterbury bells, and other blue flowers.[13]

FRANCES BENJAMIN JOHNSTON. Pavillon Colombe with *potager* in foreground, c. 1925
Prints and Photographs Division, Library of Congress, Washington, D.C.

In 1909 the music pavilion was inaugurated with a gala reception honoring the future king of Greece, a reception that rose above the usual gatherings of "discontented Americans and rather off-color French," as Walter Gay phrased it. By this time, Anne Morgan, the daughter of John Pierpont Morgan, was in residence at Villa Trianon, forming a ménage à trois that was known as the Versailles Triumvirate, which Walter Gay affectionately called "these three jolly women." Bernard Berenson was also a fan, enjoying the "flutter of Sapphic society" he found with them.[14]

Edith Wharton would have no part of that world; hers revolved around her literary and gardening friends and those in New York and Paris society. After World War I, during which she and most other American residents in Paris volunteered for war-relief charities, Wharton found a refuge in the village of Saint-Brice-sur-Fôret, ten miles from Paris, in an elegant eighteenth-century *pavillon* built for an actress and given her stage name, Pavillon Colombe. Wharton revealed in her autobiography: "As soon as I was settled in it peace and order came back into my life. At last I had leisure for the two pursuits which never palled, writing and gardening."[15]

As at Le Bréau and Villa Trianon, the principle rooms at Wharton's Pavillon Colombe opened onto a terrace overlooking the garden. A friend and frequent guest there recalled "the neatest of parterres, soberly patterned in green…and then a grove of trees, with a shadowy basin of water in the midst; and beyond again the open breadth of the *potager* where abundant flower-borders framed the trim kitchen stuff and drilled lines of fruit espaliers spread their arms."[16]

When Wharton acquired the property, she had the overgrown English-style garden cleared away and restored the parterre "à la française," as it had been documented in an old picture. Stone vases for geraniums stood along the terrace edge, and the corners of the grass parterres beyond were punctuated with topiary cones and edged with beds of pinks bordered in box. The box hedge separating the kitchen garden from the woods basin (reportedly designed for La Colombe by artist Hubert Robert) was restored and the fountain repaired.[17] Shade-loving perennials were planted beneath the trees.

The *potager*'s six rectangular beds were filled with flowers and vegetables, including sweet corn. Wharton lamented to her niece Beatrix Farrand, a noted garden designer, in 1923 that because of continuous rain only the last of three sowings of sweet corn had succeeded. She added, "But I'm going to try again!"[18] Annuals grouped by color edged the beds. One long path was lined with spectacular *Lilum candidum*, and others with a succession of orange/yellow, blue/violet, and

Wood clearing with statue at Pavillon Colombe. Beinecke Rare Book and Manuscript Library, Yale University, New Haven, Connecticut

ROBERT NORTON.
*View of the Gardens
and Garden Façade
at Pavillon Colombe*,
c. 1925.
Watercolor on paper.
Edith Wharton
Restoration, Lenox,
Massachusetts

white/pink blooms. Wharton rejoiced in gardening away from the harsh New England climate, exclaiming, "there is a foretaste of heaven in the long leisurely progression of the French summer."[19]

A beautifully planned and cared-for home and garden were essential to Wharton's well-being. A young friend revealed, "With Mrs. Wharton I was intimidated by the aesthetic perfection of everything about her. It was only over the tiniest flaws in the aesthetic appointments of her rooms, a flower faded or misplaced in a vase, that I ever saw her for a moment show distress."[20]

While work was going forward at Pavillon Colombe, Wharton spent the winter and spring of 1919 at Hyères on the Mediterranean coast, near Toulon. Here she found an abandoned convent of the Sainte Claires, built into the walls of a ruined fourteenth-century château perched on a hill overlooking the town and the sea beyond. Her friend Robert Norton explained that "her imagination was stirred by its romantic associations, by the ruined towers of the castellated peak which rose at its back…and by the old red roofs clustering around a fortress-church at its feet."[21] Wharton bought the property and began restoring the building and clearing the overgrown wilderness. A road was made and soil imported for a garden that would eventually fill twenty-eight terraces following the contours of the hill. Fortunately Wharton's novel *The Age of Innocence* (1920) was a huge success, and she would have nearly $70,000 to spend on the project.[22] In the process, she would become a formidable plantswoman, creating a personal garden that reflected her finely tuned aesthetic sense and deep-felt response to place.

Wharton was able to move into the château just before Christmas 1920. She wrote to her sister-in-law that a severe frost had blackened "all the stock-in-trade of a Riviera garden":

flowers, eucalyptus, pepper and orange trees, buddleias, and even the native wildflowers, but she took comfort in knowing "this prodigal nature will repair things in a year." She exulted that on Christmas day, "we had the divinest Riviera weather, & as we sat on the terrace in the sun taking our coffee after luncheon a joint groan of deliverance escaped us at the thought of London, New York & Paris!"[23]

The terrace overlooked the entrance road, which was lined with purple irises, prickly pear, and Judas trees. A rock garden on the west of the château had a fine collection of subtropical plants. The surrounding maquis—the native underbrush of ilex, olive, carob, juniper, cistus, rosemary, myrtle, and aloe—formed the background to the intensively cultivated terraces on the east of the château, most with a handkerchief of lawn. The terraces, enclosed in stone walls and connected with winding paths and stairs, each provided slightly different conditions, and as her expertise grew, Wharton exploited them all. An article in *Country Life* noted that she was "not satisfied with growing the ordinary routine herbaceous plants or shrubs, and in most cases her experiments are very successful.... One gets a feeling everywhere that the plants are grown for a genuine appreciation of their own individual value."[24]

The wall of one high terrace was draped with roses. Its pergola seat faced a lawn and was flanked with cypress surrounded by flowering shrubs. A large double terrace below, edged with arches of cypress, was formally planted in rows of orange trees and yel-

low freesias. Another terrace was filled with roses and another with cherries, spring flowers, and bulbs. In one shaded terrace, camellias, azaleas, and arum flourished. The walls of the terraces were draped with bougainvillea, bignonia, and other climbers, while the rocky slopes above each terrace were densely planted with both native and exotic blooms. A wealth of flowering shrubs, both common and rare, lined the paths. Wharton was fond of red/yellow/orange combinations: one narrow path was lined with orange freesias and African daisies. As well as color, she delighted in contrasts of form and texture: foxtail lilies and spiky aloes thrust out of softer planting, and a vivid orange creeper sprawled under a mass of lilac statice. Blue echium was massed with copper-colored cuphea and scarlet aloes and planted against the purple hardenbergia covering the front of the château.[25]

Wharton counted among her friends several noted gardeners. She visited Lawrence Johnston at Hidcote and, after 1924, at his garden, Serre de la Madone, at Menton. She sought his advice in designing a garden of blue flowers for Pavillon Colombe. For a rose garden of floribundas and hybrid teas there, she received help from her niece, Beatrix Farrand. In England, she made pilgrimages to the gardens of Gertrude Jekyll (where she received a rather indifferent reception) and Ellen Wilmott (where she revealed she had difficulty paying attention to the plant names).[26]

Sainte-Claire-le-Château brought Wharton a new gardening world, as well as friends with whom she exchanged plants and expertise. Her neighbor in Hyères was Charles de Noailles, who lived at the Villa Saint Bernard. Harriet Martineau, who included Sainte-Claire in her book *Gardening in Sunny Lands* (1924), visited Wharton and gave her advice. Iris Origo, whom Wharton had known since childhood, introduced her to Mary Senni, whose iris gardens at Villa Senni near Rome Wharton often visited. (In November 1931, Wharton apologized to Senni that she had left a book behind, as "I was so much interested in your garden that I entirely forgot.") Wharton agreed to contribute an article to the magazine *Giardino Fiorito*, edited by Mary Senni, and suggested that "it might be interesting to tell your readers what I have in bloom at this moment, in a large garden with poor soil, and very little of that."[27]

In the late 1920s, Wharton suffered from a series of bereavements, as well as precarious health, although she continued her exhausting schedule of travel. Her writing and her gardens sustained her. In 1933 on hearing of the death of Iris Origo's son, Gianni, Wharton wrote Mary Senni, "Life is a grim business but we must take refuge in the nearest task whatever it is, and dealing with gardens is one of the most helpful."[28]

GERALD MURPHY. *Villa America*, 1925.
Tempera and gold leaf on board.
© 2004 estate of Honoria Murphy Donnelly

This painting served as Gerald Murphy's house sign.

A new generation of Americans discovered the French Riviera in the 1920s, especially artists and writers, who came off-season, when villas could be rented cheaply. Cole and Linda Porter spent the summer of 1922 at Château La Garoup in Antibes and invited their friends Gerald and Sara Murphy, who were then living in Paris, to visit. Gerald Murphy, whose father owned the elegant Mark Cross shops on New York's Fifth Avenue and in other cities, had joined the business after graduating from Yale (where Cole Porter was a classmate). He found selling luxury goods to be deeply unsatisfying and was exasperated by a social code that discouraged a man from expressing a serious interest in literature, art, or music. As he wrote to his fiancée, Sara Wiborg, "it has been a life of such sham and unreality."[29] After marriage and the birth of their first child, Gerald moved his family to Cambridge, where he completed two years of study at the Harvard School of Landscape Architecture. The birth of two more children did not prevent the Murphys from sailing for Europe in 1921, since they intended to make their home there. (Sara, who spoke fluent French, had spent much of her youth traveling in Europe.)

After visiting gardens in England, the Murphys settled in Paris, where they immersed themselves in the modernist movement, becoming intimate with Picasso and the artists and composers associated with Diaghilev's Ballets Russes. As Gerald described it, "There was a tension and excitement in the air that was almost physical. Always a new exhibition, or a recital of the new music...or a premiere of a new play or ballet."[30] Gerald himself began to paint and enjoyed an acclaimed if all too brief career, exhibiting his precisionist abstractions in the Salon des Indépendants.

Gerald had not, however, lost his interest in gardens. Introduced to Antibes by the Porters, the Murphys bought a villa at Cap d'Antibes in 1923. Its attraction was a seven-acre garden of exotic trees collected by the previous owner, which included date palms, white-leafed maples,

Far left: Garden of Gerald and Sarah Murphy at Villa America, Antibes, c. 1925. © 2004 estate of Honoria Murphy Donnelly

Lower terrace of Villa America, with Baoth Murphy in a toy auto, c. 1925. © 2004 estate of Honoria Murphy Donnelly

and pepper trees, along with figs, olives, and lemons. The land sloped down from the house in a series of terraces that, happily, faced away from the mistral—flowers as well as trees flourished there. In remodeling the modest house, which they christened "Villa America," the Murphys added a large terrace under a massive silver linden tree and furnished it with comfortable rattan café chairs and tables for viewing the garden and the sea beyond. Sara was in charge of the herb garden, and Gerald supervised every detail of the house and grounds. As his son-in-law later wrote, "Gerald was incapable of buying, owning, or even arranging anything other than in almost perfect…style or taste."[31]

The gardens provided cut flowers for the house as well as fragrant walks. Among the exotics, Gerald grew more familiar blossoms: peonies, tulips, roses, heliotrope, jasmine, and camellias. An orchard and a *potager* supplied produce, including American favorites such as sweet corn. The Villa America became a private Eden for the Murphys, the world as it ought to be. Here they created a richly satisfying life, sharing with family and scores of friends, lovely food, beautifully arranged rooms, and flower-filled gardens. Gerald himself once revealed to Scott Fitzgerald that for him "only the invented part of life was satisfying, only the unrealistic part. Things happened to you…of course I accepted them, but…for me only the invented parts of our life had any real meaning."[32] In 1933, when reality made itself felt in the deteriorating health of their younger son and the grave financial state of Mark Cross, the Murphys left Villa America for New York, never to return.

On a visit to New York in 1920, the Murphys had been introduced to Ronald Tree, an American brought up in England, and his new wife, Nancy Langhorne Perkins. The Trees were renting architect Ogden Codman's elegant town house on East Ninety-sixth Street.[33] Codman, coauthor with Edith Wharton of *The Decoration of Houses* (1897), had moved to France in search of a more cultivated milieu than that of New York. The Trees would subsequently spend summers in England, but spring and autumn at Nancy's family home Mirador in the Blue Ridge Mountains of Virginia.

Nancy Tree's mother was the eldest of the celebrated Langhorne sisters from Virginia. Her aunt, Irene Langhorne, was married to illustrator Charles Dana Gibson, the originator of the Gibson Girl, and lived in New York. Another, Nancy Langhorne, had married Viscount Waldorf Astor and lived in England at Cliveden; in 1919 she became the first woman elected to the House of Commons. When Ronald and Nancy Tree moved to England in 1926 on Ronald's appointment as master of the Pytchley Hunt in Northamptonshire, they had immediate entrée into powerful social and political circles.

As Nancy Lancaster (her third husband was Colonel C. G. Lancaster), she did much to propagate the "English country house" style of relaxed elegance through the London firm Colefax and Fowler, which she bought in 1949. She had an equally impressive record of creating significant gardens both at Mirador and at three country estates in England.

At the first of these, Kelmarsh Hall in Northamptonshire, which the Trees leased for ten years beginning in 1928, Nancy felt right at home. The house had "the stamp of history" that she loved and, like old country estates in Virginia and villas in Italy, was surrounded by farmland rather than a park.[34] Here Nancy restored the old box gardens, clipping two yew hedges into topiary loggias, and added herbaceous borders to a path that skirted a walled vegetable

Steps to the guesthouse bordered with lavender, Villa America. © 2004 estate of Honoria Murphy Donnelly

Top: Palms in the Villa America garden. © 2004 estate of Honoria Murphy Donnelly

garden. She asked advice on planting from Lawrence Johnston's friend Norah Lindsey, as she used "a very formal layout with very informal planting. That's what I liked. And she used common plants, not rare or precious hybrids, allowing them to grow luxuriantly."[35] This had been Nancy's own planting style at Mirador. She told the story of a visit to see a celebrated border in Virginia and of learning its secret from the gardener: "I plants [*sic*] it so thick that no weeds can come up," adding, "That's what I like. Everywhere things growing through everything else."[36]

Ronald Tree bought the three-thousand-acre estate Ditchley Park with its magnificent early-eighteenth-century house in 1933, the same year he was elected to the House of Commons as a Conservative. Nancy found the estate "much too grand and formal" but nonetheless decorated the interiors brilliantly.[37] Ronald Tree had a taste for splendor. He hired designer Geoffrey Jellicoe, author of *Italian Gardens of the Renaissance* (1925), to plan a suitably grandiose treatment for the hundred-acre pleasure ground. Nancy insisted on a flower garden, however, and Jellicoe's partner Russell Page drew one up consisting of fourteen beds edged with planks (as aunt Irene Gibson's garden in Maine had been) and filled with the old-fashioned flowers Nancy loved.

Topiary chessmen at Haseley Court. Country Life Picture Library, London

After World War II, the Trees were divorced and Nancy married Colonel Lancaster, the owner of Kelmarsh Hall. This marriage was short-lived—she had perhaps married the house, not the man. In 1954 at fifty-seven (Edith Wharton's age when she embarked on her two French gardens), Nancy Lancaster found the house and garden that would become her life's work and that would embody her flair, taste, background, and years of design experience. Haseley Court in Oxfordshire was an estate built on a domestic scale and in ruinous

Folly in the center of the Walled Garden at Haseley Court, Oxfordshire. Andrew Lawson Photography

condition when she stumbled upon it. But the house had "the stamp of history," fourteenth-century remnants incorporated as the Gothic wing of a graceful eighteenth-century stone structure essentially one room deep. She completed the restoration and decoration of the house in just a year, avoiding all stiffness and formality and complementing the beautifully proportioned interiors with fine period furniture and fabrics. She was delighted that "everything from my past fit perfectly into the rooms of Haseley."[38]

The garden would take considerably longer. The entrance allée had been cut down, and the garden had disappeared in weeds and wilderness, although, miraculously, a marvelous topiary chess had survived on the south side of the house. Lancaster brought in Jellicoe to rework the entrance and forecourt with a terrace and an entrance drive planted with a double row of plane trees. Beds by the façade of the house were filled with yellow and blue plants—phlomis, lavender, and caryopteris, among others. Yellow roses and *Magnolia grandiflora* (reminiscent of Virginia) softened the house wall. Potted datura, oleanders, and lemons (redolent of Italy) decorated the terrace, which overlooked the topiary garden bordered with clipped yews and standard laurels. Parterres under the topiary chess pieces were planted with santolina, lavender, and stachys.

A small wood lay to the east of the terrace. Lancaster designed a Gothic folly, constructed of papier-mâché scored to mimic stone, as a focal point under the trees, where hellebores and Turk's cap lilies flourished. She had a fishpond enlarged into an elegant canal that paralleled the axis of the house, creating a lovely vista into the wood.

The balance of the garden evolved gradually outward from the house, which she envisioned as a series of inviting, densely planted enclosures linked by more open areas. An arch in the yew hedge beyond the terrace led into the Box Parlor, enclosed on two sides by the walls of the house. The mostly paved space was accented with box monoliths and filled with potted plants in summer. Beyond was a smaller lawn enclosure between the house wing and range of outbuildings, with a sundial in the center. The outbuildings were given their own parterre garden in front, opening onto a spacious gravel courtyard where roses and clematis were trained on the ancient stone walls.

The most enchanting, and largest, of all the garden areas was entered by an arch in the stone wall on one side of the court. Here Lancaster found the remains of a foursquare vegetable garden, walled on two sides. She had the other two sides enclosed with hornbeam tunnels to create long, shady vistas, one of them ending in a grotto with a statue and dripping water, the other in a mirror that exaggerated its length. The crossing of the paths that divided the beds was marked with a lattice summerhouse covered in roses, modeled on an old Virginia structure. She adored old roses and used them, backed with box, to border the crossing paths. For planting, she asked the advice of Graham Stuart Thomas, who suggested color modulations for the underplanting of the roses—blue/pink along one axis, yellow/red along the other. Lancaster was impatient with that sort of scheme, preferring the surprise of the unexpected in color as well as form. She found the English herbaceous border "where everything is lined up front to back by height" very boring.[39]

Lancaster's layout for the four large squares of the Walled Garden, as she put it, "sort of took shape gradually as I went along." She used box for much of the formal structure partly because "Virginian gardens had box. I love the smell of it."[40] She liked to plan on the largest possible scale with a formal design softened by exuberant planting. Two squares were reserved for vegetables and soft fruits. The square closest to the house began as a decorative *potager*. In the other, a medlar set into a lawn was circled by a path with four radiating paths to the corners of the square, and espaliered fruit trees bordered the box hedges. On the other side of the axial path, the third square was given a lawn with a scalloped border all around filled with white flowers and roses and clematis on white lattice trellises.

The design of the fourth square was based on a Roman mosaic in Venice, which Lancaster visited often, as she loved the Palladian villas of the Veneto. In the center of the square, a circle divided into wedges by spokes of golden box was planted with lavender. Four radiating paths in the form of fishhooks were edged with box; the curved shapes were accented with four weeping mulberries and further divided by box into beds for bulbs and flowers (see page 100). Lancaster never claimed to be a horticulturist, preferring "old-fashioned flowers that you saw in old gardens.... Things that I saw as a child in Virginia." (Although she had become a British subject during the war, her Southern heritage was compelling—a Confederate flag always flew at Haseley Court when she was in residence.)

For Nancy Lancaster, house and garden were linked: "I really lived in the drawing room. I would sit in there in the summertime with the doors and windows open. It was simply lovely. And you could walk right through to the garden. All of Haseley was that way." In 1974 there was a fire in the drawing room and bedroom above. Once the extensive damage had been repaired, she was forced to sell Haseley Court, retaining rent-free the Coach House and the Walled Garden. Her wry comment to her biographer, "I was born in a cottage, and it seems as though I'm going to end my life in one" proved true, although she would enjoy her marvelous Walled Garden for twenty years more before her death at ninety-six.[41]

Nancy Lancaster's contemporary Peggy Guggenheim was devoted to art rather than gardens, although she would have a significant garden at her palazzo in Venice. Guggenheim had inherited a fortune from her father, who had gone down on the *Titanic*, and in 1921 she left New York for Paris. She wrote, "At this time I was worried about my virginity. I was twenty-three and found it burdensome. All my boyfriends were disposed to marry me but they were so respectable.... " She married American artist Laurence Vail, who had accommodated her in Paris, and gave him two children before beginning the long sexual odyssey that she recounted with relish in her autobiography.[42] With one of her lovers, English poet Douglas Garman, she made a garden at Yew Tree Cottage in Sussex. When he refused to marry her in 1937, she revealed, "I went out into the garden and tore up his best flower bed. It contained many rare plants and I...hurled them over the fence into the field next door. It happened to be the coldest night of the year."[43]

At the time, Peggy Guggenheim had embarked on her career as a major collector and supporter of contemporary art, opening a gallery in London in 1938. During the war, her influential Art of This Century gallery was located in New York. She confessed, "Much as I loved Art of This Century, I loved Europe more than America, and when the war ended I couldn't wait to get back." Postwar London had no appeal, and in any event her two beloved Lhasa apsos would have been quarantined for six months. Venice had not suffered war damage and, as Guggenheim wrote, "you have a tremendous sense of freedom in Venice in general, tremendous. You can wear any clothes you want and walk everywhere you want. No automobiles to run over you." In 1947 she rented the top floor of the Palazzo Barbaro from the Curtis family and the next year bought the Palazzo Venier dei Leoni across the Grand Canal as a permanent home for herself, her dogs, and her now impressive collection of contemporary art, which had just been shown at the Venice Biennale.[44]

Peggy Guggenheim in the garden Palazzo Venier dei Leoni, Venice. Peggy Guggenheim Collection, Venice (The Solomon R. Guggenheim Foundation, New York)

The palazzo, begun in 1748, had never been finished beyond the first floor, but it had, as she noted, "one of the largest gardens in Venice, with very old trees." The palazzo was given a modern white interior and a flat roof on which the new owner liked to sunbathe in the nude. The garden, centered on a decorative wellhead circled with columns and crowned with iron latticework, was refurbished and a massive Byzantine marble seat, on which she delighted to pose with her dogs, was added. Although the English roses she planted did very well, Guggenheim was more interested in the garden for its use as an entertainment and exhibition space than for its horticultural attractions. When one of her grandsons asked her what she liked most to do, she replied, "The best thing is to make love in the garden."[45]

Guggenheim's early support of contemporary painting and sculpture was an indirect cause of the appointment of art historian John Rothenstein to the directorship of the Tate Gallery in London. In 1938 she had organized an exhibition of works by Arp, Brancusi, Duchamp-Villon, Calder, and other avant-garde sculptors for her London gallery. As many of the pieces were brought from France, they had to be certified as works of art rather than bronze, wood, or stone industrial materials, which were subject to duty. James Mason, then director of the Tate and the authorized expert, dismissed them as "not-art."[46] The resulting furor over his incompetence led to his dismissal and the hiring of John Rothenstein.

Before beginning his career as a museum director, Rothenstein had taught a course on modern art at the University of Kentucky at Lexington. Here he met Elizabeth Smith, an aspiring painter, and they were married in 1929. After returning to England with his new wife, John Rothenstein headed museums in Leeds and Sheffield before being appointed director of the Tate in 1938. This was no sinecure. He, Elizabeth, and their daughter, Lucy, crowded into an apartment at the Tate that he described as "our dank, beleaguered flat, half-underground." He added, "a house in the country had become the condition of any ability to surmount the series of hardships that prevailed at the Tate, and the multifarious plots that arose every day."[47] They were ecstatic to be able to buy the Old Rectory and three acres of overgrown garden in the rural village of Newington, Oxfordshire, in 1951.

Renamed Beauforest House after the last abbot before the 1546 dissolution of nearby Dorcester Abbey, the stone house had a Georgian façade, but a sixteenth-century back next to the Norman parish church. The grounds, which sloped down to the river, retained a line of spindly columnar yews, ancient trees, a Victorian nut walk, and the remnants of a foursquare garden defined by a cruciform pattern of ragged box. In planning additions to the garden, the Rothensteins had both the advice and the physical help of a professor at Oxford, Father Vincent Turner. Elizabeth developed a passion for old roses and ordered 120 varieties from the nursery where Graham Stewart Thomas had grown his

Folly in the garden of Beauforest House, Newington, Oxfordshire. Curtice Taylor

collection. Nearly two hundred trees and innumerable shrubs were added. Elizabeth's trained sense of color and shape and Father Vincent's talent for free-form design resulted in distinctive planting with no herbaceous borders, which Elizabeth disliked, or garden rooms. Father Vincent insisted on "not making rooms. It is much more difficult and satisfying to design open-plan and achieve unity."[48]

The lawn between the house and river was backed with a curved planting of roses and shrubs, such as gold-leafed spiraea, purple cotinus, and variegated euonymus. *Stachys lantana*, hostas, hellebores, peonies, and foxgloves—another of Elizabeth's passions and one that she allowed to seed everywhere—filled spaces around the shrubs. A path from the lawn through the screening yews, now topped and clipped, led to the four irregular rectangles formed by the box hedges. Here, in what could have been a formal parterre, Elizabeth and Father Vincent created a geomorphic abstraction of rounded shapes, spiky forms, sweeping lines, and accents of hot color.

One rectangle centered on a birdbath surrounded with box, gold-leafed *Lonicera*, and variegated euonymus clipped into buns, and overflowing with roses, including the self-sown lesser maiden's blush, which dated from early in the garden's history. The hybrid tea called Mr.

Opposite: Columns and rose chains, Beauforest House. Curtice Taylor

Birdbath and clipped box, Beauforest House. Curtice Taylor

Lincoln was included because Abraham Lincoln was born in Kentucky. Another rectangle was filled with viburnum and perennials with purple or yellow leaves. The third was centered on a Lawson cypress and the fourth on a Colorado spruce, both of them surrounded with roses. A wrought-iron dome on concrete pillars, a copy of one designed by Elizabeth's grandfather in Kentucky, marked the crossing of the two paths dividing the rectangles. A line of matching pillars supported looped chains with sweeps of climbing roses. The adjacent nut walk was extended with a pergola for clematis and more roses and planted with spring flowering bulbs.

John Rothenstein himself took no part in the planning and planting of the garden, but he dedicated himself to weeding, which he found very therapeutic. He confessed that "Beauforest was not only a creation of beauty that grew with every month; it was a haven of sanity from the lunacy of my official life in these years, and its serenity nourished us continuously."[49] Happily, John Rothenstein was knighted for his work at the Tate and retired to Beauforest House in 1968. ❧

Hollywood House, Adare, Limerick, Ireland. Curtice Taylor

Chapter Six

Americans choose to live abroad today for many of the reasons that motivated expatriation in the past. Some stay in Europe because of marriage, others for careers; a fortunate few have second homes abroad, and many still settle there because only in Europe can they find a sympathetic environment in which to live and work. The gardens they have made demonstrate as well some of the same desires and impulses that motivated the creation of earlier gardens abroad.

In the eighteenth century, many young women accompanied their new husbands to England as did George Washington's first love, Sally Fairfax. Two hundred years later, in 1986, Carla Heffner, who had grown up in a small Mississippi town, married Sir Kenneth Carlisle and went to live at Wyken Hall, a sixteenth-century manor surrounded by a thousand-acre farm in rural Suffolk. Carla's route to England was more roundabout than that of Sally Fairfax. A veteran of civil-rights activism and Vietnam War protests, Carla worked as a journalist in Washington, D.C., and later apprenticed at the Chez Panisse restaurant in San Francisco before traveling to Burgundy to learn viniculture. She moved to Paris, and at thirty-eight went on to London, where she met Sir Kenneth, who was struggling with his farm at Wyken. Carla Carlisle's arrival brought Southern warmth and ease to both house and garden and sparked the farm operation with American enterprise. First to succeed was a seven-acre vineyard that within five years had produced an award-winning wine. Next was a top-notch restaurant featuring the six Wyken wines and a shop for distinctive crafts, which were quickly followed by a

Rose Garden at Wyken Hall, Stanton, Suffolk. Curtice Taylor

Right: Gothic bench, Wyken Hall. Curtice Taylor

Saturday market for local produce. Meanwhile, she had produced both a son and a weekly column chronicling her experiences at Wyken for *Country Life* magazine.[1]

Diversification became evident in the house and garden, as well as on the farm. The rather gloomy half-timbered manor was lime-washed an assertive red known in Elizabethan times as Suffolk pink. Pleached apple trees were planted along the façade to serve as a living verandah with rocking chairs lined up underneath. This is part of what Carla Carlisle calls the Brooch Garden (paid for with her husband's fortieth-birthday gift of a diamond brooch), which enlivens the gravel turnaround in front of the house. The rockers, several Gothic benches, and the house window frames were painted a lilting American blue. She wrote, "I inherited my grandmother's dislike of white garden furniture, a feeling I shared with Nancy Lancaster who said 'it looks like aspirin in the garden.'"[2] Other decorative additions were the cast-iron gate of corn stalks and ears, copied from one in New Orleans; a bench with an ogee arch that Carla calls her "Bellini bus shelter"; and a splendid dog house—in the guise of a carpenter Gothic chapel painted blue with red trim—which hides the fuel tanks that supply the Aga cooking stove.

When he took over Wyken from his parents in the late 1970s, Sir Kenneth discovered that he had a passion for gardening. (This was not surprising, as his mother was the daughter of Lord

Aberconway, and he had spent his childhood at Bodnadt in Wales. His great-grandparents had
owned Château La Garoupe and its garden on Cap d'Antibes, which was later rented in summers to Elsie de Wolfe and the Cole Porters, among others.) At Wyken Sir Kenneth filled the
meadow in front of the manor with spring bulbs and flowers and replaced herbaceous borders
at the back with formal, hedge-enclosed herb and knot gardens to tie together the three sections of the house. A pergola led from the replanted areas to a new rose garden. His wife slyly
commented, "I suspect there is an inverse connection between hormone levels and horticultural passion," but she was soon caught up in garden-making as well. She wrote, "I have lived in
three countries, but I feel that the immigrant and the gardener have this in common: long tap
roots which seek nourishment deep beneath the surface of the earth."[3]

Wit and whimsy as well enliven her substantial improvements to the garden. The shop
office, painted red with blue trim, was given its own cottage garden, entered through a red-

painted gate made of crossed spades and pruning shears. An edible garden for soft fruits and asparagus was added next to the kitchen wing of the house, enclosed with lattice for climbers and centered on a huge copper planter weathered to the blue of the house trim. On the same axis, she planted double "red hot" perennial borders, which lead through the corn gate to the croquet lawn. In a gesture toward America, she used wisteria as standards in the rose garden, as fence drapery, and as a covering for the flint-and-iron gazebo that was a wedding present. An anniversary gift of earrings was exchanged for an avenue of limes connecting the garden to the woods; a diamond watch paid for the pond beyond the rose garden, where Adirondack chairs are positioned on the pier for duck watching.

Carla Carlisle's passion for peacocks and for dark Brahmas, an elegant breed of fowl, demanded the construction of appealing small houses—one hen house exterior is decorated with American license plates. The adjacent vegetable garden was spruced up with rectangular beds, columnar yews, three painted totems, and an enclosing fence of woven willow. A dog cemetery for deceased Labradors was enclosed with a yew hedge. (The new wildlife area

Kitchen garden, Wyken Hall. Curtice Taylor

beyond is affectionately known as Yellow Dog National Park.) Her most recent projects are the restoration of a farm cottage as a writing studio and, for the restaurant, the development of a beer named Good Dog, because in her words "it makes you want to sit and stay!"[+]

Another trans-Atlantic marriage that resulted in an appealing garden was that of Ann Letchworth, who had gardened in Bedford, New York, before her marriage to Englishman Anthony Huntington. She moved with him in 1982 from London to the Old Rectory in the Northamptonshire village of Sudborough. Her friends warned her that she would soon be bored, as she was not a horsewoman, but instead she began a garden on the three-acre grounds that became a ruling passion. In the process, Ann Huntington has gotten to know many notable gardeners and become a knowledgeable plantswoman herself. Rosemary Verey designed a glorious walled *potager* for her with brick paths separating box-edged squares and rectangles for vegetables and herbs, with espaliered peaches along the wall. Metal craftsmen from a neighboring village made tunnels that cover the walks and the ornamental arbor covered with roses, clematis, and kiwi that stands in the center.

A long vista in the garden runs from a stable courtyard, where an ancient apple is entwined with Seagull rose, through the *potager* and the naturalistic planting of willows, birches, spring bulbs, and hellebores beyond, to an elegant wooden bridge that crosses the pristine trout stream at the bottom of the garden. On the other side, a path skirts a pasture filled with sheep and meanders through a wood, the habitation of rabbits, badgers, and pheasants.

Intensively planted, deep, curving borders flank the lawn that opens out from the house. These are Ann Huntington's creation and her domain, their ongoing improvement aided by advice from designer Rupert Golby. From the drawing-room windows, a vista of roses, perennials, flowering shrubs, and ancient trees (including a John Cabot acacia) leads to a pond with

Lake at Hollywood House. Curtice Taylor

Walled *potager*, Hollywood House, Limerick. Curtice Taylor

the sheep meadow in the distance. She had wanted masses of rhododendron, Japanese maples, and other acid-loving plants she had grown in Bedford, but the limestone soil prevented it. Instead, she has concentrated on David Austin roses and hellebores, both planted in impressive variety and depth, and on collecting unusual flowering shrubs and perennials.[5]

A garden made recently in the Republic of Ireland began in much happier circumstances than that of Cornelia Adair in the nineteenth century. A Georgian manor, Hollywood House, and its surrounding two-hundred-acre farm in County Limerick was an anniversary present from Carolyn Lynch to her husband, Peter, whose great-grandparents had come from Ireland to live in New England. Carolyn thought the slower pace and the smaller scale of Ireland, together with the pleasures of rural life, would be a welcome change for her husband. The estate offered woodland, open fields, and the appeal of gardening in the equivalent of U.S.D.A. zone 9, far warmer than zones 5 and 6 in Massachusetts. In a mostly deforested country, the abundance of century-old trees representing more than fifty species, planted by previous owners of the estate, was compelling to these lovers of New England forests.

In planning the gardens, the Lynches consulted American designer Channing Blake, who laid out terraces around the house and made two lakes. The Irish designer Jim Reynolds was called in after Blake's death to design the kitchen garden and orchard and to enlarge the flower gardens. Carolyn Lynch, however, has taken the lead in planning, having gardened for years in Massachusetts. Bridle paths around the property for walking, jogging, and bicycling, as well as horseback riding, were a priority, as was a collection of American trees that reflect the tastes of the present owners, much as the old trees had reflected those of previous owners. (Ireland has only four native trees.) She rejoices in a climate that allows her to grow a number of broad-leafed evergreens that are new to her, as well as old favorites. A separate arboretum near the lake in front of the house is gradually filling with exotics, including cork, olive, fig, camellia, and tree ferns. She admits that "everywhere I go, I see a tree I want, and I go wild as I can grow almost everything here."[6]

Carolyn Lynch has literally put her imprint on the stone terrace to the south of the house. Designed to link the house with the walled gardens in the rear, the terrace was laid out with gray limestone blocks that she found too austere, so she knocked holes in them for low-growing plants. (She is not entirely joking when she says that her favorite garden tool may be a hammer!) Boxwood lines the walk here and forms a leitmotif throughout the gardens. On the terrace overlooked by the drawing room windows, two beds for summer annuals are bordered in box, and there is a Celtic knot in box that has been enlivened by infilling with crushed hot-red brick. In a rectangular pool meant for lilies, Lynch has planted box, the growing tips clipped at different heights to suggest water. She explains that she had enough of the real thing in the Irish weather, but she kept the sound of water with a fountain made from a mushroom stone that stands in the midst of the box.

The walled vegetable garden behind the house has become a perennial garden with four large rectangles bordered in box and working greenhouses against the north wall. The same plants flourish here that grow in her garden in Massachusetts, but over a season of six rather than three months. She is a real collector and wants every variety of a plant she loves. She confesses, "I can't do perennials on a small scale—I love the big plants." The vegetables now occupy a large area beyond the flower garden, but here too flowers and interesting plants are infiltrating. Roses thrive on the south wall of the cattle barn. Carolyn Lynch comments: "Depending on the way the wind is blowing, the smell can be either/or!"

American millionaires still covet castles, as did industrialist Andrew Carnegie, who bought Skibo Castle in Scotland in 1898. In 1994 entrepreneur Bob Van Kampen and his wife bought the fifteenth-century castle Hampton Court set on a thousand acres at Hope-under-Dinmore in Herefordshire. They chose not to restore the gardens remaining from

Stone terrace, Hollywood House. Curtice Taylor

Victorian times but commissioned English designer Simon Dorrell to create a series of new areas acknowledging the past. One walled garden holds vegetables; another is a tribute to the Arts and Crafts Movement, with twin octagonal pavilions beside a canal. There is a rose parterre laid out as a sixteenth-century knot, an herbaceous border in the style of Gertrude Jekyll, and an avenue of limes characteristic of seventeenth-century English gardens. A maze with a tower in the middle invites contemplation.

These gardens are recognizably English, albeit with an American accent. The Garden of Cosmic Speculation, begun in the 1980s by American architect Charles Jencks and his late wife, Maggie Keswick, on her family property in Scotland is emphatically contemporary. Jencks admits, "We both got fed up with English garden design and English gardens. How many ideas are there in contemporary landscaping?"[7] Jencks, an exponent of Postmodernism, drew on recent discoveries in physics for his vocabulary of sculptural earthworks, spiraling water features, and wooden constructions. The results are visually beautiful as well as provocative, focused on ideas rather than plants. A four-hundred-foot-long, sinuously terraced hill (explicating the theory of folding), and a sixty-foot-high spiral mount (based on the double helix of DNA) loom over shaped planes of water. The Black Hole incorporates an elongated shape patterned in fractals, and nearby is the Symmetry Break terrace, which is built into the curve of a ha-ha. The vegetable garden contains constructions symbolizing the senses. Distinctive wrought iron gates with twisted bars representing waves of energy separate areas of the garden.

American artists also still garden abroad. Distinguished abstract painter John Hubbard grew up in Connecticut, lived in Japan, and studied at the Art Students League in

The Foursquare Garden, Chilcombe House.
Curtice Taylor

New York before leaving for Europe in 1958. Three years later, he settled on the Dorset coast, which has permeated his lyrical expressionist paintings of coastlines, estuaries, rivers, rocks, trees, and hills. In 1969 John and his English wife, Caryl, bought seventeenth-century Chilcombe House near Bridport in Dorset, where they have reared their two children. The stone manor sits on the top of a south-facing slope that looks out onto rolling hills. Prominent garden features included two gigantic Irish yews across the lawn from the central door of the manor and a stone foundation wall a few steps down from the lawn. The first garden at Chilcombe was made beyond the wall, divided by an axial path, and enclosed with a tapestry hedge of holly, copper beech, and hornbeam. The space to the left was divided into four large beds with a cross axis leading to the cobble garden on the right of the path. This geometric arrangement suggested to John Hubbard a medieval *hortus conclusus*. "I was mainly thinking of Books of Hours and pictures of gardeners working below stone buildings... the shape of the garden replicating the shape of the house. That is how I envisioned it and it just grew by stages."

Hubbard has vivid memories of his parents' garden in Connecticut, which he describes as "typically American in that they made much of the surrounding woods, native plants like ground-pine and lady's slipper and a very American rock garden.... I adored every square inch of it, made my own patch of annuals as a small boy, and can still recall its ground-plan." He has visited a number of notable English gardens but says he has only stolen "a few modest ideas," such as Hidcote's tapestry hedge.[8]

The planting of the four large squares in the first garden, and indeed the planting of the spaces that spread outward, overtaking the vegetable garden and orchard beyond the tap-

The *potager*, Chilcombe House. Curtice Taylor

Top: Medlar in the Cobble Garden, Chilcombe House. Curtice Taylor

estry hedge, reflected both John Hubbard's growing horticultural knowledge and his artist's vision. "As my interest in and experience of plants evolved, always in tandem with Caryl, more pieces were planted up, the aim replicating my painting's use of close-up, layering, repetition, contrast. Edges, rectangles and such relate to the picture frame and both grass and cut edges act as foils to apparent abandon."[9] There are a few borders, but hardly conventional ones. The central grass path of the foursquare garden is punctuated at either end with fastigiate (naturally spired) Irish yews and lined with roses. There are no plants in drifts, but rather arrangements of colored and textured forms that ascend as well as overflow the beds. Acacias, witch hazels, and poplars, low-clipped mounds of box and juniper, unusual nightshades, salvias, and other tender perennials. Both American natives and interesting varieties of old favorites, such as eupatorium, thalictrum, helianthemum, allium, liatris, persicaria, and lysimachia, are integrated into living compositions of rewarding complexity.

In the cobble garden (so called for the path of cobblestones that bisects it), the planting is lower, though no less imaginative. The two gardens are joined by a grass path that begins at a stone seat with a clipped yew as a back, passes under a rustic arbor, and ends in a sculpture. Beyond the tapestry hedge, through a clipped arch, the former vegetable garden is now filled with flowers, although Hubbard always finds room here to grow sweet corn. Other enclosed garden rooms center on a brilliant blue urn and a sundial. A bank of thyme spills over a low wall separating levels, while roses, clematis, and tender climbers cover arbors and walls. Hubbard's studio windows face away from the floral splendor. He notes that, because he works constantly in the garden, "I found it impossible to achieve that state of detachment required in order to use it as a source for art."[10]

John Hubbard's contemporary Mark Rudkin grew up in Fairfield, Connecticut (his mother named her fledgling bakery Pepperidge Farm after the family estate), and studied painting in New York before switching to dance and touring Europe with Martha Graham's troupe in 1954. Like George Lucas one hundred years earlier, Rudkin fell in love with Paris and remained there when the troupe returned to New York. Rudkin also began a new career in France, but as a landscape designer rather than as an art dealer. First Rudkin made his own garden in Le Mesnil-Saint-Denis, near Paris, on a six-acre property he bought in 1970. After building a low modern house and a painting studio, he turned his attention to the grounds, a slope with a few rhododendrons, camellias, and an overgrown field. He began by adding more camellias, rhododendrons, dogwoods, and other flowering trees and shrubs, carpeting the ground beneath with ferns, primroses, and other shade lovers he had known in Connecticut. A gravel path winds down the slope to the field now filled with spring bulbs.

Across the field, an opening in a hornbeam hedge leads to an unexpected series of formal garden rooms separated by hornbeam and beech hedges. Within a square divided into two unequal rectangles by a grass allée and a cross axis ending in a Renaissance wellhead, each compartment is distinctive. The largest is a double parterre with clipped box edging beds where roses share space with foxgloves, delphinium, and sedum Autumn Joy. Another section holds a raised, rectangular rock garden. Two square areas, bisected by stone paths, are devoted to mauve and pink flowers and to white ones. A further rectangle is bisected into two squares, one of which has mauve and pink flowers and the other white flowers. A larger square divided by trellises holds blue flowers, with masses of asters, which Rudkin loves. He notes, "I put in big flowering plants that foam and explode and fall to the ground. I like to use large blocks of color and not get them all mixed up together like scrambled eggs."[11]

Mark Rudkin's garden drew the attention of a board member of the Museum of French-American Cooperation at Château de Blerancourt in Picardy, and he was commissioned to make a garden there in 1989. His design used American plants in his characteristic massed color blocks for late summer and fall flowering. Separated into two sections by a hedge, the hot color area includes helianthus, helenium, heleopsis, and oenethera. The blue and mauve section features asters, eupatorium, and phlox, among other flowers. At the museum, Rudkin has recently designed another garden adjacent to the autumn one, for April and May bloom in blue and white perennials and shrubs.

In 1992 Rudkin received a commission to plant the grounds of the Musée Américain in Giverny. On one side of the museum, he made a poppy meadow, a favorite subject of Monet and the American Impressionists. He trained white wisteria on the metal arbors covering the central walkway and the outdoor terrace, added lavender edging, and filled a large bed with clipped balls of santolina, heliotrope, and limonium. On the other side, he created a series of garden rooms filled with other reliable fragrant plants. In the same year, he was commissioned by the French cultural minister to design the planting for the refurbished Palais Royal in Paris. The garden there had been a favorite meeting spot in the eighteenth century and it is just as popular today, thanks to Rudkin's raised beds of fragrant annuals surrounding four paved spaces for sitting and lingering under the double row of linden trees.

Edith Wharton cogently observed that for the French, "the enjoyment of beauty and the exercise of the critical intelligence are two of the things best worth living for." She continued, "every Frenchman and every Frenchwoman takes time to live, and has an extraordinarily clear and sound sense of what constitutes *real living*," concluding that "life is an art in France."[12] The attention given to the quality of everyday life and to the art of dining well has been a revelation to Americans living in France. Thomas Jefferson, for example, soon after his arrival in Paris, apprenticed his servant James Hemmings to a caterer to learn French cookery and began amassing a fine collection of wine.

Two hundred years later, in 1980, journalist Patricia Wells went to Paris with her husband, Walter, who had become an editor for the *Herald-Tribune*. Since her childhood she had dreamed of living in Paris, where she was to immerse herself in the world of food and professional chefs. Her first book, *The Food Lover's Guide to Paris* (1984), reflected her long study and passion for the ingredients, places, and personalities that make France a culinary treasure house.[13]

In the same year, Susan Hermann arrived in Paris for a year's course at La Varenne cooking school and became Patricia Wells's assistant. She returned to France in 1994 with her husband, sculptor Michael Loomis, and they bought an old, half-timbered house, a former convent beside the church in Louviers, Normandy. The small garden behind the house had apple and pear trees, hydrangeas and roses. To separate it from the parish land, they planted a row of espaliered apples with a hedge of shrub rose along part of the boundary. Hermann added herbs and a *potager* for vegetables and annual flowers. There was no room for corn, however. She laments: "There are few American foods that we miss, but corn on the cob is one and until recently it was nearly impossible to find."[14]

Patricia and Walter Wells had meanwhile bought an eighteenth-century farmhouse perched on a hill in Provence. In her book on life there, Patricia acknowledged that Provence "opened our eyes, our ears, our sensibilities to the rituals of French daily life in the countryside" and asked, "did this place have a magic way of magnifying ordinary pleasures?"[15] The magic comes not only from the bounty of local produce—olives, figs, grapes, apricots, cherries, mushrooms, and truffles, all sorts of vegetables, a variety of game including wild boar, delectable cheeses, and meats—but also from the stark beauty of the *garrigue* region—arid hills covered in fragrant evergreen and gray-leafed shrubs—and the sensuous appeal of cultivated farmlands, lavender fields, olive plantations, and vineyards.

New gardens made in Provence reflect both aspects of the countryside, many influenced by the brilliant designs of the late Nicole de Vesian and Alain David Idoux.[16] Gourmet food

Lawn terrace,
Le Clos Pascal,
Menerbes,
Provence. Solange
Brihant

merchant Eli Zabar and his wife, Devon Fredericks, friends of the Wellses, often visited
Provence and had gotten to know Nicole and Alain who lived nearby. In 1992, when the Zabars
bought a defunct restaurant on two and a half terraced acres nestled against the looming walls
of the hill town Menerbes, they asked Nicole de Vesian for advice. They had admired her modest garden in nearby Bonnieux, made from the plants of the region—rock rose, broom, thyme,
juniper, box—with sage, rosemary, santolina, and other aromatics clipped into mounds and
arranged as sculpture between dry stone walls. Stone balls and vertical cypress provided accents.

Before any garden could be made at Le Clos Pascal (named for the restaurant), the terraces
had to be cleared, their walls repaired, and the restaurant remodeled into a home for an
American family accustomed to large rooms and plenty of baths. A spacious summer kitchen/
living room overlooking the hills was built to accommodate the two serious cooks. The entrance
to the main garden terrace is between the house and summer kitchen, and it was only here that
Devon insisted on a lawn for a play area, with a tree house for the Zabars' twin sons.

Devon relates that de Vesian was excited by the site, which was very much like that of her
own garden, and she began by making "stories," as she put it, out of the existing elements. An

Steps in lower garden, Le Clos Pascal.
Solange Brihant

ancient gnarled pine leaning over a wall was given four large parasol pines below for visual support. Elsewhere solitary pines were augmented with smaller ones and, together with the plane trees and acacias on the main terrace, they provide dramatic contrasts of light and shade with sharply defined shadows. Nicole de Vesian echoed this geometry of light with her characteristic sculptural shapes of stone and clipped aromatics.

The access drive from the road below transverses the lower terrace, where stone stairs mount the hill to the house. A small olive plantation occupies the upper terrace, with a *potager* on the terrace below, easily accessible from the kitchen. Here there are espaliered apples and pears, as well as cherry trees that provide fruit for juice, jam, and tarts. The olives are pressed into oil, and a planting of lavender provides oil as well. The Zabars delight in the intense flavors of the produce—what their garden lacks, they find in the local markets—and they relish the sense of being really away from New York. They do *not* grow sweet corn, since Devon believes that "you shouldn't take your world with you."[17]

Atlanta industrialist Holcombe Green and his wife, Nancy, also fell in love with Provence and embraced the way of life possible there. In 1992 they bought the rundown Mas de Pilons with its 160-acre farm near Saint-Rémy. The selling point was a magnificent view of the craggy mountain range, the Alpilles, beyond the fields in front of the farmhouse. The restoration of the house took five years, and the garden has grown exponentially from Holcombe's first planting in 1995 of aged olive trees in four large squares of germander and santolina beyond a rectangular reflecting pool. In the evolution of the garden, the Greens have had the help of English designer Tim Rees, but Holcombe, a perfectionist who always has "a grander strategy," as he says, has taken the executive position.[18]

An allée of ancient plane trees leading to the house was continued along the drive outside the gate by transplanting mature trees. The view of the Alpilles was underlined by row upon row of lavender (ten thousand plants clipped into balls!), a six-acre field of wildflowers beyond (reseeded at the end of each summer), and an olive plantation. An unsightly power line pylon was hidden behind a twenty-foot mound planted with fifty fully grown trees, its undulating profile echoing that of the distant mountain range. More than one thousand trees have been planted elsewhere on the property.

Inspired by Dutch designer Jacques Wirtz, Holcombe commissioned a topiary garden beside the house with mature box, yew, and holly clipped into fanciful shapes flanked by allées of live oak. A hydrangea walk leads to the gardens behind the house. The Greens have long collected contemporary art, and Holcombe has a special fondness for the sculpture garden, which is laid out in clipped box parterres that focus the gaze on both figurative and abstract examples. A rose garden filled with favorites such as Guy de Maupassant, Claude Monet (enormous cream and pink blossoms), and climbing *mutabilis* leads from the original pool garden to the

Top: Sculpture garden at Mas de Pilons, Saint-Rémy-de-Provence. Solange Brihant

Bottom: Olives, Mas de Pilons. Solange Brihant

potager. Here pomegranates are underplanted with rosemary and box-edged beds are filled with French vegetables, as well as spring bulbs, summer annuals, and vines. Holcombe enjoys using local materials both indoors and out. Ancient stone columns, finials, wall fountains, and urns decorate the gardens, and a splendid pergola constructed with thirty columns from an old manor separates the topiary and sculpture gardens.

The Amalfi coast and the Sorrento peninsula of Italy shelter American writers today as

Topiary garden, Mas de Pilons. Solange Brihant

they did when novelist Marion Crawford lived there in the nineteenth century. A precipitous road winds up the mountains from Amalfi to Ravello. From the cathedral square at the top, a quarter-mile footpath leads to La Rodinaia, the home of author Gore Vidal and his partner, Howard Austen. The house is aptly named the Swallow's Nest, as it clings to the side of Ravello's highest hilltop, which is surmounted by the ancient Villa Cimbrone and its garden. The villa was an eleventh-century estate, Cimbronium, which was bought in 1904 by Ernest Beckett, Lord Grimthorpe, who made a garden filled with pavilions, fountains and sculpture. Lord Grimthorpe's daughter built a house on the lower ledge of the villa garden in 1925, with four levels that open onto terraces overlooking the sea far below. In 1972 Gore Vidal bought the house and its grounds, which are filled with olive groves, figs, chestnut, and lemon trees, as well as stone pine, cypress, and ilex.[19]

Vidal's visions for the property have expanded and contracted as his gardeners have coped with the stony soil, hot summers, and lack of rain. First to go was the lawn, which was replaced with a welcome swimming pool and patio. Vidal invited a landscape architect for a long stay in the 1980s, and her efforts convinced Howard Austen that he would need to pay much more attention to the garden, so he has taken over its planting and supervision. He installed an irrigation system himself, but even so relies on plants that thrive in Southern Italy. Hydrangea, iris, gaillardia, dianthus, agapanthus, fuchsia, and tritoma, as well as roses, wisteria, and bougainvillea, are among those supplying bloom in the intensively cultivated portions of the property. Geraniums cascade from planting boxes on the terrace and along paths. Thyme, rosemary, and broom thrive in sunny spots, and naturalized cyclamen flourish under the trees. An allée of cypress lines the long entrance path, and another borders stone stairs leading down toward the sea.

The garden continues to develop. Several years ago Vidal wrote elatedly, "I have just come from the *cisterna* above the house, set in a jungle that a team of gardeners is clearing away, revealing old walls, paths, rare trees—a whole new property with rich earth. The air intoxicates.

We are in a planting mood."[20] Although Vidal does not write in his garden, as Marion Crawford did, he spends precious hours walking through the cool green of the woods, savoring the scents and colors of the flowers, and reading by the pool or on one of the terraces, surrounded by the blue expanse of sea and sky.

The art, culture, and landscape of Italy have been irresistible lures for American artists since Benjamin West's pilgrimage there in 1760. Two hundred years later, painter Maro Gorky, daughter of the American Expressionist Arshile Gorky, and her husband, sculptor and writer Matthew Spender, abandoned London for the hills of Tuscany. Here, in an eighteenth-century farmhouse on thirty-two acres, they follow their vocations in close collaboration with the land. The garden, Maro Gorky's province, provides food for the table, as well as aesthetic challenges analogous to painting. As she puts it: "The intention is to create order out of chaos, yet it's exciting when things don't go as you plan and the medium itself answers back."[21]

In 1980 painter Sheppard Craige settled nearby, in San Giovanni d'Asso, and embraced the austere, undulating hills, and limitless horizon in his landscapes. Over the last decade, however, he has abandoned paint and canvas for the living materials of wood, earth, and water to create a continuously expanding garden of ideas within a ten-acre wood called La Ragnaia (a place to catch birds). Like Thomas Jefferson at Monticello, Craige removed only superfluous undergrowth, leaving the mature evergreen oak and occasional pines, cypress, and poplars, as well the violets, iris, and hellebores in residence. Both the sensual aspects of the place—the play of light and shadow, the contrasts of textures, the subtle variations of color, the dialogue between plants and structure—and reflections on the experience are integral to his vision.

The entry to the garden is through a "Great Circle in the form of an oval," an area of grass centering on a particularly numinous oak. Stairs from a viewing platform, the Throne of

Sheppard Craige by the Fountain of Good Sense,
La Ragnaia, San Giovanni d'Asso, Tuscany

Top: JOELLYN DUESBERRY, *Sheppard's Garden, Tuscany*, 1997.
Oil on linen, Private collection

the Woods, navigate a precipitous drop of one hundred feet. Descending, a visitor passes the Fountain of Good Sense, the first test of which, according to Craige, is not to drink from it! Further on, a column is surmounted by a box containing a carpenter's level, mason's plumb, and compass called the Little Tabernacle of the Big Certainties, i.e., gravity and electromagnetism.[22]

Moving water as a counterpoint to the rustling of leaves and patterns of light and shade plays an important role; a visitor is always conscious of the splash or trickle from the five basins in the garden. It was just five years ago, however, that Sheppard Craige mastered the complex system of holding tanks, pipes, pump, solar panels, and valves that make it possible. As a villager remarked after seeing Craige struggling with his hoses, "If you send water downhill, all the saints will help you; if uphill, only money will help you!"

The level area at the bottom of the slope accommodates a parterre garden around the oak trees. Craige may have had in mind the formal symmetries of his mother's flower garden in Virginia, but the four large rectangular beds, with patterns of box and laurel and a groundcover of ivy and hellebore, are bordered in volcanic tufa blocks rather than box. These locally cut blocks form the basic unit of the garden, and since they are laid with no cement, they can be moved or removed at will. The Pavilion of Nothing—four wood beams rising from the corners of a twelve-foot square bed filled with box—marks the crossing of the two axial paths. Within the beds, playful manipulations of geometric shapes occur as Craige shifts blocks in an ongoing dialogue with the garden.

The scale of the garden, both physical and metaphysical, is evident only with exploration, for pathways, inscriptions, objects, and seats invite strolling and reflection. A path enclosed by laurel hedges leads north from one axis to a stone seat in the woods, passing the Center of the Universe, a circle of columns open to the sky inscribed "Only here / Only now / Only this / Only as it

La Ragnaia, San Giovanni d'Asso, Tuscany

is." The other axis extends east beyond the parterre between laurel hedges to an enclosed oval, which is floored in ivy and roofed in oak boughs. In the other direction, the axis extends 150 feet to a raised terrace with a bench inscribed "Divini Gloria Ruris" that provides a viewing spot down the length of the garden.

An inclusiveness and generosity of spirit as well as space characterize the garden. La Ragnaia has traditionally been accessible to all visitors. In the fall, residents used to gather acorns to feed the pigs and, as the name La Ragnaia implies, to hunt birds and small beasts. Now villagers are encouraged to visit, linger, and (inevitably) comment on the ongoing project so unlike a traditional Italian garden. Several of the older boys provide after-school and summer help, while their grandmothers come often to sit on the thoughtfully placed benches and enjoy the play of light and shade and the sound of water. ❧

Notes

INTRODUCTION

1. Timothy Mowl, *Gentlemen and Players: Gardeners of the English Landscape Garden* (2000), 39–40.

2. Interview June 11, 2001. Frank Cabot has written about his garden in a book noteworthy both for its sensitive text and for the beauty and range of its photographs: Francis H. Cabot, *The Greater Perfection* (2001).

CHAPTER ONE

1. See Peter Martin, *The Pleasure Gardens of Virginia from Jamestown to Jefferson* (Princeton: Princeton University Press, 1991), xxii–xxiii.

2. Jefferson had acquired Shenstone's collected *Works* (1764) after his graduation from William and Mary.

3. William L. Beiswanger, "The Temple in the Garden" (1983), 170.

4. R. P. Maccubbin and Peter Martin, eds., *British and American Gardens in the Eighteenth Century* (1984), 98, and George C. Rogers Jr., "Gardens and Landscapes in Eighteenth Century South Carolina," 151–52.

5. Leigh Hunt, *The Autobiography of Leigh Hunt*, I (1903), 100.

6. Now called *The Skater*, the painting is in the collection of the National Gallery of Art, Washington, D.C. James Thomas Flexner, *Gilbert Stuart* (1955), 98.

7. Alan Burroughs, *John Greenwood in America 1745-1752* (1943), 50.

8. Information courtesy Deborah Rothwell, Museum of New Zealand.

9. *Letters and Papers of John Singleton Copley*, letter of 1775 quoted in Richard Kenin, *Return to Albion* (1979).

10. "With a bold hand, a master's touch and I believe an American heart, he attached to the Ship the stars and stripes. This, I imagine, was the first American flag hoisted in England." Winslow Watson, ed., *Men and Times of the Revolution* (1856), 176.

11. Watson, *Men and Times of the Revolution*, 143.

12. Lester J. Cappon, *The Adams-Jefferson Letters*, I (1959), 177, 228.

13. Robert C. Alberts, *The Golden Voyage* (1989), 122, 136.

14. Ibid., 162–63, 363.

15. Elizabeth McLean, "Town and Country Gardens in Eighteenth-Century Philadelphia," (1983), 143.

16. Mary Gay Humphries, *Catherine Schuyler* (1897), 188. Elopement was not unusual at the time; three of Angelica's four sisters arranged their marriages in this fashion.

17. Archibald B. Shepperson, *John Paradise and Lucy Ludwell* (1942), 63.

18. David McCullough, *John Adams* (2001), 355.

19. Letter to John Page, May 4, 1786, Papers 9:445 quoted in William Howard Adams, *The Paris Years of Thomas Jefferson* (1997), 115.

20. Quoted in McCullough, *John Adams*, 358.

21. Washington Irving, "Rural Life in England," *The Sketchbook of Geoffrey Crayon* (1819).

22. See wood engraving published in *The Lady's Newspaper* (March 1848). Before his premature death in 1834, Bates's son had aided his father in "suggesting and superintending the execution of improvements in the grounds and buildings." *Tribute of Boston Merchants to the Memory of Joshua Bates* (1864), 45.

23. Edwin P. Hoyt, Jr., *The House of Morgan* (1966), 62.

24. "Dover House, Roehampton," *Gardeners' Chronicle* (Nov. 5, 1892), 557.

25. Oct. 15, 1785, to John Bannister.

26. Was this sour grapes? Nabby Adams had accompanied her mother to Europe, resulting in the breakup of the romance.

27. Watson, *Men and Times of the Revolution*, 88.

28. John Sanderson, *The American in Paris* (1839), 104.

29. Sanderson, *The American in Paris*, 212. Elkanah Watson in 1777 had found the Palais Royal "a mass of moral corruption," 91.

30. John Vanderlyn to Peter Vanderlyn [1796], John Vanderlyn Papers, Archives of American Art, film 1040. Vanderlyn's magnificent panorama of Versailles occupies its own room at the Metropolitan Museum of Art, New York.

31. Watson, *Men and Times of the Revolution*, 92–93.

32. She was a great beauty even in her late fifties. The writer Bernard de Fontenelle when nearing the age of one hundred reportedly exclaimed on seeing her, "Oh, to be seventy again!" Claude-Anne Lopez, *Mon Cher Papa: Franklin and the Ladies of Paris* (1966), 247.

33. Quoted in Gervase Jackson-Stops, *An English Arcadia, 1600–1990* (1992), 92.

34. Another dear friend, Madame Brillon, wrote Franklin, "You combine with the kindest heart, the soundest moral teaching, a lively imagination, and that droll roguishness which shows that the wisest of men allows his wisdom to be perpetually broken against the rocks of femininity." Quoted in David Schoenbrun, *Triumphs in Paris: The Exploits of Benjamin Franklin* (1976), 349.

35. Watson, *Men and Times of the Revolution*, 87.

36. Martindale, "Benjamin Franklin's Residence in France," *Antiques* (August 1977), 271.

37. Dora Wiebenson, *The Picturesque Garden in France* (1978), 89–90.

38. Howard C. Rice, Jr., *L'Hôtel de Langéac: Thomas Jefferson's Paris Residence* (1947), 98, 113.

39. Jefferson to Cosway, Oct. 12, 1786, quoted in Rice, *L'Hôtel de Langéac*, 111.

40. William Howard Adams has called this an "amorous little theme park" with its entrance through a grotto flanked by two naked satyrs. *The Paris Years of Thomas Jefferson*, 245.

41. Cappon, *The Adams-Jefferson Letters*, 57.

42. Sept. 17, 1787, quoted in Adams, *The Paris Years of Thomas Jefferson*, 190.

43. Adams believes that the simplified plan was Jefferson's attempt to give the garden greater unity (ibid., 55). Rice calls the more elaborate plan the "finished study," Jefferson's change from the formal French style to a fashionable, irregular one (*L'Hôtel de Langéac*, 25).

44. Gouverneur Morris, *A Diary of the French Revolution* (1888).

45. William Carey Duncan, *The Amazing Madame Jumel* (1935), 176–80.

46. Sanderson, *The American in Paris*, 219.

47. Adeline Trafton, *An American Girl Abroad* (1892), 236.

48. Harvey Levenstein, *Seductive Journeys* (1998), 100.

49. John Joseph Conway, *Footprints of Famous Americans in Paris* (1912), 146.

50. Lillian M. C. Randall, *The Diary of George A. Lucas* (1979), 24.

51. George Stillman Hillard, *Six Months in Italy*, II (1847), 220.

52. Van Wyck Brooks, *Dream of Arcadia* (1958), 2, and letter of Jan. 6, 1773, in *Letters and Papers of John Singleton Copley and Henry Pelham 1739–1776* (1914), 194.

53. Izard was subsequently appointed by the Continental Congress as envoy to the court of the Grand Duke of Tuscany in Florence, but he never got further than Paris.

54. Nathalia Wright, *American Novelists in Italy* (1965), 45.

55. Rembrandt Peale, *Notes on Italy written during a tour in the years 1829-1830* (1831), 5, 186, 209.

56. An American, *Rambles in Italy in the Years 1816–1817* (1818), 355.

57. Henry Tuckerman, *A Memorial to Horatio Greenough* (1853), 36.

58. Sylvia E. Crane, *The White Silence* (1972), 123.

59. Catherine W. Pierce, "Francis Alexander" (1953), 42.

60. Mabel Dodge Luhan, *European Experiences* (1935), 412, 415.

61. Leon Edel, ed., *Henry James Letters*, II (1975), 55, 58.

62. Carol M. Osborne, "Lizzie Boott at Bellosguardo" (1992), 188.

63. Susan Hale, ed. *Life and Letters of Thomas Gold Appleton* (1885), 196.

64. Brooks, *Dream of Arcadia*, 90.

65. Laura E. Richards and Maude Howe Elliott, *Julia Ward Howe*, I (1916), 268.

66. Maude Howe Elliott, *My Cousin F. Marion Crawford* (1934), 17.

67. Nathaniel Hawthorne, *The Marble Faun* (1859). Kenyon and Hilda, unlike Story and Powers, elect to return to America.

68. Henry James, *William Wetmore Story and His Times* (1906), 74.

69. Mary E. Phillips, *Reminiscences of William Wetmore Story* (1897), 97, 171.

70. John Murray, *A Handbook of Rome and Its Environs* (1869), quoted in Sherwood, *Harriet Hosmer American Sculptor 1830–1908* (1991), 257.

71. Sherwood, *Harriet Hosmer*, 79.

72. Hawthorne, *Notebooks*, October 1858, quoted in Sherwood, *Harriet Hosmer*, 211.

CHAPTER TWO

1. Eugenia Brooks Frothingham, *Youth and I* (1938), 22.

2. Lilian Whiting, *Italy the Magic Land* (1910), 113.

3. Letters to William James, Oct. 30, 1869, and April 9, 1873, quoted in Fred Kaplan, ed., *Traveling in Italy with Henry James* (1994), 111, 121. Since the 1976 publication of Dean MacCannell's *The Tourist*, tourism has been viewed as a paradigm of modernity in its search for reality and authenticity in foreign locales and pre-industrial cultures.

4. Henry James's Roman notebook (1873) quoted in Kaplan, *Traveling in Italy with Henry James*, 188.

5. Whiting, *Italy the Magic Land*, 135–36. Charles Platt in his *Italian Gardens* (1897) noted the neglect of the Medici garden, 45.

6. Nathaniel Hawthorne, *The Marble Faun* (1859), 59.

7. Maitland Armstrong, *Day Before Yesterday* (1920), 208.

8. Helen Haseltine Plowden, *William S. Haseltine* (1947), 132.

9. Mary King Waddington, *Italian Letters of a Diplomat's Wife* (1905), 237. At her death, Mrs. Field left an estate of several million dollars. See *New York Times*, Feb. 19, 1897, 7, and June 21, 1910, 1.

10. Waddington, *Italian Letters of a Diplomat's Wife*, 53.

11. Ibid., 263.

12. Francis Augustus MacNutt, *A Papal Chamberlain* (1936), 66.

13. Ibid., 213.

14. Plowden, *William S. Haseltine*, 107.

15. Ibid., 174.

16. Ibid., 184.

17. Maude Howe Elliott, *Roma Beata* (1904), 28.

18. Richards and Elliott, *Julia Ward Howe*, II, 242.

19. Elliott, *Roma Beata*, 63, 80, 334.

20. Douglas Shand-Tucci, *The Art of Scandal* (1998), 58.

21. Elliott, *My Cousin F. Marion Crawford*, 128.

22. Phoebe Cutler, "Villas of Rome and Gardens at Home" (2000), 6.

23. Elliott, *Roma Beata*, 57.

24. Letter to Mrs. Waldo Story, June 17, 1899, in Edel, *Henry James Letters*, IV, 107. Crawford was living as a bachelor, as he and his wife had separated in 1891.

25. Walter Crane, *An Artist's Reminiscences* (1907), 129, and Elihu Vedder, *The Digressions of V* (1910), 248.

26. Edwin Cerio, *The Mask of Capri* (1957), 112.

27. Charles De Kay, "A Villa in Capri" (1902), 91.

28. Faith Compton MacKensie, *As Much As I Dare* (1938), 232–33.

29. Maryle Secrest, *Between Me and Life* (1974), 130.

30. Ralph Alan McCanse, *Titans and Kewpies* (1968), 167.

31. "The Lure of the Golden Bowl" (1983), 118. Jerome's *Aspects of the Study of Roman History* (1923) is still cited today.

32. Pliny, letters to Gallus and Domitius Apollinaris, *Epistles*, ii, 17 and v, 6, translated in Alfred Church, *Pliny's Letters* (1872), 131–38.

33. Rusticus, "A Letter to Pliny the Younger Relating to the Villa Castello" (1902) 349–54.

34. Regina Soria, *Elihu Vedder* (1970), 231–33.

35. Susan Rather, "Rome and the American Academy" (1992), 215.

36. Soria, *Elihu Vedder*, 239.

37. H. Buxton Forman, "An American Studio in Florence" (1884).

38. Ronald G. Pisano, *A Leading Spirit in American Art: William Merritt Chase, 1849–1916* (1983), 138.

39. Mabel Dodge Luhan, *European Experiences* (1935), 81. She would marry twice more and settle finally in Santa Fe, New Mexico, where she wrote her four-volume autobiography.

40. Ibid., 86.

41. Ibid., 138–42.

42. Ibid., 143–45.

43. Arthur Acton's son, Sir Harold, left the villa and its Renaissance-inspired garden to New York University, and it is now a center for Italian studies.

44. Luhan, *European Experiences*, 296.

45. A. Richard Turner, *La Pietra* (2002) 36–40.

46. Ibid., 44.

47. William Dean Howells, *Venetian Life* (1866), 94.

48. Ibid., 98.

49. Ibid., 399, 407.

50. Henry James, *Italian Hours* (1909), 69.

51. Michael Meredith, ed., *More Than Friend* (1985), xxxiv.

52. In 1881 four young American artists, Harper Pennington, Julian Story, Ralph Curtis, and Charles Forbes, taking advantage of Browning's frequent presence in Mrs. Bronson's salon, had held a group portrait sitting there. Meredith, *More Than Friend*, 6.

53. James Rennell Rudd, *Social and Diplomatic Memories, 1894–1901* (London: Edward Arnold and Company, 1923), 44.

54. Julia Cartwright, *A Bright Remembrance* (1989), 288.

55. Leon Edel, *Henry James Letters*, III, 196, and Henry James, *The Wings of the Dove* (1902; New York: Random House, 2003), 450. Claude Monet had stayed at the Palazzo Barbaro in 1909 and painted the Grand Canal from the water gate.

56. Meredith, *More Than Friend*, 170, and Edel, *Henry James Letters*, IV, 451, and III, 180.

57. Charles Quest-Ritson, *The English Garden Abroad* (1992), 95. He suggests, "The inspiration for some of Gertrude Jekyll's most successful plantings may be traced to this garden."

58. Frederic Eden, *A Garden in Venice* (1903), 24.

59. Ibid., 109.

60. Interview with Patricia Curtis Vigano, June 29, 2002.

61. Shand-Tucci, *The Art of Scandal*, 182.

62. T. "The Villa Sylvia, the Property of Mr. Ralph Curtis" (1910), 92–95.

63. *The Letters of Bernard Berenson and Isabella Stewart Gardner* (1987), 484, 495.

64. Mrs. Philip Martineau, *Gardening in Sunny Lands* (1924), 166–68.

CHAPTER THREE

1. William H. Gerdts believes that Harrison's *In Arcadia* of 1885 (Musée d'Orsay, Paris) derives from nude studies made in Grez and Concarneau in Brittany. See "The American Artist at Grez" (2000), 272.

2. Another Grez romance was between Frederick Delius and the Swedish painter Jelka Rosen. Jelka Delius related that Caroline Bruce "had a life size nude statue of the baker in Grez. This nasty statue stood in her sitting room in a corner with its back to the public so as not to show his sex, altho she had modeled this part in great detail." Lionel Carley, *Delius* (1983), 408.

3. Photocopies of Vonnoh's correspondence courtesy Mrs. Robert Rowe Thompson.

4. Marie de Mare, *G. P. A. Healy* (1954), 269.

5. Henry Bacon, *Parisian Art and Artists* (1883), 211.

6. Nesta R. Spink, *James McNeill Whistler Lithographs from the Collection of Steven Block* (2000), 14.

7. Henry James, *The Ambassadors* (1903; Ware, England: Wordsworth Editions, 1992), 118. Howells had said to Sturgis, "Oh, you are young, you are young—be glad of it; be glad of it and live…. This place makes it all come over me. I see it now. I haven't done so—and now I'm too old. It's too late." Quoted in Edel, *Henry James*, IV, 150.

8. Sadikichi Hartman, *A History of American Art*, I (Boston: L. C. Page, 1901), 225–26.

9. Lilla Cabot Perry, "Reminiscences of Claude Monet from 1889 to 1909" (1927).

10. Mary Koopman, "Giverny," quoted in Nicholas Kilmer, *Frederick Carl Frieseke* (2001), 85.

11. The Metropolitan Museum of Art, *Monet's Years at Giverny* (1978), 25, 28.

12. Louise Jones DuBose, *Enigma* (1963), 63.

13. William H. Gerdts, *Monet's Giverny* (1993), 87. Yvonne was the model for this painting of a girl sewing in a garden, now in the Corcoran Gallery of Art, Washington, D.C.

14. Ibid., 109.

15. Washington, D.C., Smithsonian Institution, Archives of American Art, MacMonnies papers, typescript courtesy William H. Gerdts.

16. Emma Bullet, "MacMonnies the Sculptor" (1901), courtesy William H. Gerdts.

17. Will H. Low, "In an Old French Garden" (1902), 9–11.

18. Sara Dodge Kimbrough, *Drawn from Life* (1976), 69, 77.

19. Frederick MacMonnies had missed the birth of his second daughter to go to the bedside of his mistress, who gave him a son. The MacMonnies's third child, a boy, died in 1901.

20. Clara MacChesney, "Frieseke Tells Some of the Secrets of His Art" (1914), 7.

21. Able Warshawsky, *The Memories of an American Impressionist* (1908), 97.

22. MacChesney, "Frieseke Tells Some of the Secrets of His Art," 7.

23. Aileen O'Bryan, "Seven Gardens," unpublished memoir quoted in Kilmer, *Frederick Carl Frieseke*, 33, 87.

24. Ibid., 89.

25. MacChesney, "Frieseke Tells Some of the Secrets of His Art," 7

26. Kilmer, *A Place in Normandy* (1997), 35–36.

27. Robert and Henri Carvallo, *Le Château de Villandry* (1998), 13.

28. For example see Brent Elliott, *Victorian Gardens* (1986), 63–64, and May Brawley Hill, *Grandmother's Garden* (1995).

29. Quoted in David Ottenwill, *The Edwardian Garden* (1989), 130.

30. A cogent account of the American colonization of Broadway is Coe Kerr Gallery, New York, *Sargent at Broadway, The Impressionist Years* (1986), with essays by Stanley Olson, Warren Adelson, and Richard Ormond.

31. Elaine Kilmurry and Richard Ormond, eds., *John Singer Sargent* (London: Tate Gallery, 1998), 116.

32. Quoted in Richard Ormond, "Carnation, Lily, Lily, Rose," in Coe Kerr Gallery, *Sargent at Broadway*, 66.

33. Stanley Olson, "Sargent at Broadway," in Kilmurry and Ormond, *Sargent at Broadway*, 20.

34. Washington D.C., Smithsonian Institution, Archives of American Art, Millet papers, reel 849, frames 964-66.

35. "Abbot's Grange and Russell House, Broadway, Worcestershire" (1911), 61. Abbey married and moved in 1880 to Gloucestershire, where

Sargent often joined him. Millet went down on the *Titanic* in 1912.

36. In her memoirs, Anna revealed that they had been in love for years, but Merritt would not ask her to marry him as he was poor and Anna's family was wealthy. Her father lost his business to fire in 1876, and they were married. Galina Gorokhoff, *Love Locked Out* (1982), 115.

37. Ibid., 163. In "A Letter to Artists," Merritt wrote, "The chief obstacle to a woman's success is that she can never have a wife." *Lippincott's Monthly* (March 1900), 469.

38. Gorokhoff, *Love Locked Out*, 184, and Anna Lea Merritt, *A Hamlet in Old Hampshire* (1902), 68.

39. Anna Lea Merritt, *An Artist's Garden* (1908), ix.

40. See Wendy Hitchmough, *Arts and Crafts Gardens* (1998), 77–84.

41. Gorokhoff, *Love Locked Out*, 184.

42. Merritt, *A Hamlet in Old Hampshire*, 63–69.

43. Merritt, *An Artist's Garden*, 22, 87.

44. Ethne Clarke in her study of Hidcote suggests that both died of tuberculosis. *Hidcote: The Making of a Garden* (1989), 11.

45. Johnston was only able to gain access to Gertrude Winthrop's income and the control of Hidcote when she was declared incompetent in 1925. Her estate at her death the following year was worth several million dollars. Doubting Johnston's financial acumen, Mrs. Winthrop had left him only the income from a portion of it, the rest going to a niece. Ibid., 64.

46. Clarke speculates that Johnston enlisted "to take him away from his mother's smothering devotion." Ibid., 14.

47. Johnston was an amateur painter; his large tapestry-like canvases still hang at Hidcote. Ibid., 25.

48. See Hill, *Grandmother's Garden*. There is a 1908 watercolor by George Elgood of a similar garden at Raunscliffe, Leicestershire illustrated in Gertrude Jekyll and Lawrence Weaver, *Arts and Crafts Gardens* (1912), 160.

49. Clarke (*Hidcote*, 55) notes that Johnston had requested a leave in 1913 to visit Italy and may have firmed his plans for this long avenue by studying Renaissance gardens there.

50. For a thoughtful analysis of the garden's creation and a tour of the garden's corridors and rooms through the seasons, see Anna Pavord, *Hidcote Manor Garden* (1993).

51. Clarke, *Hidcote*, 49. Mrs. Winthrop's garden was given a brick-paved center circle with a sundial. Johnston had the sundial removed from the Phlox Garden and the center paved.

52. Mary Anderson de Navarro, *A Few More Memories* (London: Hutchinson, 1936), 186. Alfred Parsons designed a garden in 1895 for the de Navarros at Court Farm, Broadway.

53. Vita Sackville-West, "Hidcote Manor" (1949), 476, 478.

CHAPTER FOUR

1. The 1915 edition of *Titled Americans* listed 454 American women with European titles. This popular annual had begun publication in New York in 1890.

2. Richard Kenin, *Return to Albion* (1979), 139.

3. Constance Smedley, "The American Colony" (1907), 494.

4. Gertrude Atherton, *American Wives and English Husbands* (1898), 143–44.

5. Ibid., 184–85.

6. Hesketh Pearson, *The Marrying Americans* (New York: Coward, McCann, 1961), 151. Helena subsequently married the earl of Kintore, and the duke married another American, Kathleen Dawes.

7. Smedley, "The American Colony," 493. The most flagrant example of conspicuous expenditure occurred with the marriage of Consuelo Vanderbilt to the ninth duke of Marlboro in 1895. Her father settled a yearly income of $2.5 million on the couple and provided $10 million for the rehabilitation of Blenheim. This marriage ended in an annulment in 1921, and both remarried. Consuelo Vanderbilt's autobiography is tellingly titled *The Glitter and the Gold*.

8. G. C. Taylor, "The Borders at Floors Castle" (1930), 761.

9. J. L. Garvin, *The Life of Joseph Chamberlain* (1933), 366.

10. Peter T. Marsh, *Joseph Chamberlain* (1994), 319.

11. Garvin, *The Life of Joseph Chamberlain*, 369.

12. "The Right Hon. J. Chamberlain—His Home and Garden," *Journal of Horticulture*, 32 (March 12, 1896), 232. On an 1896 visit to the Endicott Peabody home, Glen Magna in Danvers, Massachusetts, Chamberlain put his expertise to use in laying out an enclosed Italian garden adjoining the old-fashioned flower garden there. Mary's mother, Ellen Peabody Endicott, a keen gardener, had inherited the property in 1892. In 1926 she was awarded the Hunnewell Gold Medal from the Massachusetts Horticultural Society.

13. Richard Harding Davis, *About Paris* (1895), 200. Henry James in *The American* explores this theme in reverse.

14. Ruth Brandon, *A Capitalist Romance: Singer and the Sewing Machine* (1977), 187.

15. Ibid., 214.

16. At the prince de Polignac's funeral, Paris Singer met dancer Isadora Duncan and they became lovers, living at The Wigwam, where Paris remodeled the gardens after those at Versailles. Ibid., 218–19.

17. Suzanne Rodriguez, *Wild Heart* (2002), 91.

18. Ibid., 180.

19. Peter McGowan Associates, *Crathes Castle Historical Landscape Survey* (1997), 18. Courtesy Callum Pirnie, head gardener.

20. Eileen A. Bailey, ed., *Crannog to Castle* (2000), 66–67.

21. J. J. Joass, "On Gardening: with Descriptions of Some Formal Gardens in Scotland," *The Studio* (1897).

22. George S. Elgood and Gertrude Jekyll, *Some English Gardens* (1905), 43–44.

23. In 1926 Crathes was inherited by Sir Robert's nephew James, who, with his wife, Sybil, is largely responsible for the appearance of the garden today.

24. Johanna Johnston, *Mrs. Satan* (1967), 255, and Barbara Goldsmith, *Other Powers* (1998), 440.

25. The garden was described in the London *Express and Journal* as filled with "rare and gorgeous plants." Quoted in Johnston, *Mrs. Satan*, 285.

26. Ciaran O'Keeffe, *The History of Glenveagh* (1991), 24–27.

27. Michael George and Patrick Bowe, *The Gardens of Ireland* (Boston: Little, Brown, 1986), 176-7.

28. Guest book at Glenveagh Castle, courtesy Sean O'Gaoithin, head gardener.

29. Ibid.

30. O'Keeffe, *The History of Glenveagh*, 31. Mrs. Porter was the gardener. She planted single dahlias from American seeds that still reappear in the *potager*.

31. Henry P. McIlhenny, "Glenveagh Castle, County Donegal" (1986), 100.

32. Ibid., 101.

33. Ibid. Letters from Lanning Roper beginning 1970 in the estate office, Glenveagh.

34. One of the more printable comments from the *New York Sun* stated, "Apart from his money, Astor is one of the weakest aspirants who ever stood the suffrages of a New York constituency." Quoted in Lucy Kavaler, *The Astors* (1966), 175.

35. Ibid., 191.

36. Kenin, *Return to Albion*, 196.

37. The impressive ruins of Pompeii were not far from Astor's Sorrento villa.

38. Ottenwill, *The Edwardian Garden*, 164.

39. Quoted in Judith Flanders, *A Circle of Sisters* (2002), 237.

40. Ibid., 261. Kipling referred to her as the "Ways and Means Committee."

41. It was the Garden Conservancy's Christmas greeting in 2002.

42. "Bateman's, Sussex, the Residence of Mr. Rudyard Kipling" (1908), 231.

43. Bernard Berenson, *Aesthetics and History in the Visual Arts* (1948), 84.

44. *The Letters of Bernard Berenson and Isabella Stewart Gardner*, 481. Berenson wrote Mary in this year, "I would like you to take great, great pleasure in being with me, in keeping house for me. I would like you with spontaneity and eagerness to put me first in everything." Ernest Samuels, *Bernard Berenson* (1987), 121.

45. Ibid., 141.

46. *The Letters of Bernard Berenson and Isabella Stewart Gardner*, 495.

47. Samuels, *Bernard Berenson*, 225.

48. Iris Origo, *Images and Shadows* (1970), 88.

49. Ibid., 18, 116. Her American grandmother in 1927 provided the six-mile-long pipeline to supply the water that made the garden possible.

50. Caroline Moorehead, *Iris Origo* (2000), 160. The magazine's fifteen issues had 120 subscribers.

51. An article on Ninfa, published several years after Marguerite Caetani's death, details her planting. Lord Skelmersdale, "The Gardens at Ninfa, Italy," *Journal of the Royal Horticultural Society* (June 1969), 246–52.

52. William Weaver, "A Legendary Italian Garden" (1997), 13.

53. Quoted in Moorehead, *Iris Origo*, 286.

54. Marie Clews's first husband was Robert Goelet, the brother of May Goelet, the duchess of Roxburghe. Clews's wedding gift to Marie was the life-size skeletal bronze *God of Humormystics*, holding a rose in his hand and crushing a toad under his left foot; it still stands by the entrance to the château.

55. Henry Clews, *Mumbo-Jumbo* (1923), quoted in Marie Clews, *Once Upon a Time at La Napoule* (1998), 5.

56. This is a fascinating account that remakes what must have been a supremely difficult marriage into an artistic and spiritual collaboration.

CHAPTER FIVE

1. H. Montgomery Hyde, *Henry James at Home* (1969), 86.

2. Edel, ed. *Henry James Letters*, IV, 63.

3. Hyde, *Henry James at Home*, 92.

4. Edel, ed. *Henry James Letters*, IV, 114.

5. Edith Wharton, *A Backward Glance* (1933), 245.

6. Edel, ed. *Henry James Letters*, IV, 300. In this year James wrote about Wharton, "She is too pampered & provided & facilitated for one to be able really to judge of the woman herself, or for her even, to be able to get really at things." Edel, *Henry James*, V, 208.

7. Margaret Terry Chanler, *Autumn in the Valley* (1936), 116. Daisy Chanler, the daughter of Louisa Crawford and Luther Terry and half-sister of Marion Crawford, had grown up in Rome.

8. William Rieder, *A Charmed Couple* (2000), 54, 41. This very entertaining double biography is based on Matilda Gay's pungent diaries and illustrated with Walter Gay's paintings.

9. Washington, D.C., Smithsonian Institution, Archives of American Art, Walter Gay Papers, letter from Walter to Matilda Gay, June 2, 1914, and Walter Gay, *Memoirs* (1930), 61.

10. Rieder, *A Charmed Couple*, 73, and Samuels, *Bernard Berenson*, 65.

11. Rieder, *A Charmed Couple*, 115–16.

12. Alfred Allan Lewis, *Ladies and Not-so-gentle Women* (2000), 191.

13. Elsie de Wolfe, *After All* (1935), 148, 165–66.

14. Rieder, *A Charmed Couple*, 116, 118.

15. Wharton, *A Backward Glance*, 363. She had become ill in the course of her strenuous war work, for which she was awarded the Legion of Honor.

16. Percy Lubbock, *Portrait of Edith Wharton* (1947), 138.

17. Eleanor Dwight, *Edith Wharton* (1994), 220. This delightful, illustrated, and thoroughly researched biography gives a circumstantial account of both of Wharton's gardens in France.

18. R. W. B. Lewis, ed. *The Letters of Edith Wharton* (1975), 474.

19. Ibid., 218–19, and Wharton's manuscript "Gardening in France," Beinecke Library, Yale University.

20. Lubbock, *Portrait of Edith Wharton*, 163–64.

21. Quoted in Dwight, *Edith Wharton*, 239.

22. Lewis, *Edith Wharton*, 430. The novel won the Pulitzer Prize.

23. Lewis, ed., *The Letters of Edith Warton*, 436–37.

24. E.C., "A Riviera Garden" (1928), 612.

25. Harriet Martineau, *Gardening in Sunny Lands* (1924), 174–76.

26. Wharton, *A Backward Glance*, 250, and Lewis, ed., *The Letters of Edith Wharton*, 473.

27. Nov. 18 and Dec. 13, 1931. Transcripts of Wharton's letters to Mary Senni from 1931 to 1937 courtesy Patrick Chasse. The Wharton manuscripts for the articles "December in a French Riviera Garden" and "Spring in a French Riviera Garden" are in the Beinecke Library, Yale University.

28. May 13, 1933. Courtesy Patrick Chasse.

29. Calvin Tompkins, *Living Well Is the Best Revenge* (1962), 23.

30. Ibid., 33.

31. Honoria Murphy Donnelly, *Sara and Gerald* (1982), xi.

32. Aug. 20, 1935, ibid., 100.

33. The Trees also met Elsie de Wolfe this winter and attended receptions at the house she shared with Bessie Marbury in New York. Robert Becker, *Nancy Lancaster* (1996), 113–14.

34. Ibid., 155.

35. Ibid., 176. All of Nancy Lancaster's gardens are analyzed by Martin Wood in a four-part series (Winter 1998), 50–62; 49 (Spring 1999), 43–57; 50 (Summer 1999), 28–42. Surprisingly, in his acknowledgements, Wood does not cite Becker's biography, much of it in Nancy's own words based on many interviews, although he quotes her from it.

36. Becker, *Nancy Lancaster*, 371.

37. Ibid., 192.

38. Ibid., 343. I am indebted to the current owners of Haseley Court, Mr. and Mrs. Desmond Heyward, who invited me to visit both house and garden, still beautifully kept, and shared their recollections of Nancy Lancaster.

39. Ibid., 371.

40. Ibid., 370.

41. Ibid., 355 and 382.

42. Peggy Guggenheim, *Out of this Century* (1946), quoted in Anton Gill, *Peggy Guggenheim* (2001), 84.

43. Guggenheim, *Out of this Century*, 155. In his introduction to the 1979 revised edition of her autobiography, Gore Vidal amusingly comments, "I began to see Peggy Guggenheim as the last of Henry James's transatlantic heroines, Daisy Miller with rather more balls."

44. Ibid., 319, 426. Bernard Berenson visited the exhibit and asked Peggy why she collected such things. She responded that she couldn't afford old masters. He replied, "You should have come to me, my dear, I would have found you bargains." Gill, *Peggy Guggenheim*, 371.

45. Guggenheim, *Out of this Century*, 333, 392.

46. Gill, *Peggy Guggenheim*, 198.

47. John Rothenstein, *Brave Day, Hideous Night* (New York: Holt, Rinehart and Winston, 1967), 343, 153. I am indebted to Carol Newman for putting me in touch with her friend Lucy Rothenstein Dynevour, still in residence.

48. Tony Venison, "From Rectory to Roses," *Country Life*, 182, no. 24 (June 16, 1988), 154.

49. Rothenstein, *Brave Day, Hideous Night*, 343.

CHAPTER SIX

1. The columns were collected in *South-Facing Slope* (2001). Articles on Wyken Hall have appeared in *House & Garden* (April 1998) and *Victoria* (May 2002). The son's name is Sam Fenimore Cooper Carlisle.

2. Carla Carlisle, *South-Facing Slope*, 8.

3. Ibid., 160, 29.

4. Interview, March 23, 2002. I am grateful to Carla for a most entertaining visit.

5. My thanks to Ann and Tony Huntington for their gracious reception. An article on the Old Rectory appeared in the English edition of *House & Garden* (June 1993).

6. Phone interview April 16, 2003. My thanks go to estate manager Peter O'Shaughnessy for a very informative tour of the gardens.

7. Owen, "Twists and Turns" (1998), 350.

8. Letter to the author, Dec. 6, 2002.

9. Ibid.

10. Ibid.

11. Stephen Whitlock, "An American Grows in France" (1999), 72.

12. Edith Wharton, *French Ways and Their Meaning* (1919), 71, 110, 112.

13. Davis Halberstam, "A Wonderful Life" (2000), 298.

14. Susan Hermann Loomis, *On Rue Tatin* (2000), 154. Susan Loomis runs a cooking school in her house.

15. Patricia Wells, *At Home in Provence* (1998), 11. Patricia Wells holds cooking classes in Provence, as well as in Paris.

16. See Louisa Jones, *Gardens in Provence* (1992), and Page Dickey, *Breaking Ground* (1997), for Alain David Idoux.

17. Interview, March 15, 2003.

18. Holcombe and Nancy are noted for their marvelous meals at Mas des Pilons, a French extension of their characteristic Southern hospitality. I was there most recently in June 2002 for lunch and a tour of the garden, still a work in progress.

19. I enjoyed a memorable visit with Gore Vidal and Howard Austen on Sept. 5, 2001, and experienced at first hand the breathtaking beauties as well as the difficulties of the site. Sadly, Howard Austen died in 2003 and Gore Vidal decided to leave La Rodinaia to live in California.

20. Gore Vidal, *Palimpsest: A Memoir* (New York: Random House, 1995), 143.

21. Catherine Fairweather, *La Dolce Vita* (2001), 96.

22. Names of garden areas are from Sheppard's delightful "Rapid Guide" to the garden available on his Web site www.laragnaia.com. See also May Hill, "La Ragnaia, an Artist's Garden in Tuscany," *Hortus*, 14, no. 4 (Winter 2000), 38–44.

Bibliography

"Abbot's Grange, and Russell House, Broadway, Worcestershire, the Residence of Mr. F. D. Millet," *Country Life* (January 14, 1911): 54–61.

ACTON, Harold. *Memoirs of an Aesthete 1939–1969*. New York: Viking Press, 1970.

ADAMS, William Howard. *The Paris Years of Thomas Jefferson*. New Haven: Yale University Press, 1997.

AHRENS, Kent. "Pioneer Abroad: Henry R. Newman (1843–1917), Watercolorist and Friend of Ruskin." *American Art Journal* 8 (November 1976): 85–98.

ALBERTS, Robert C. *The Golden Voyage: The Life and Times of William Bingham 1752–1804*. Boston: Houghton Mifflin, 1989.

AMERICAN, An. *Rambles in Italy in the Years 1816–1817*. Baltimore: N.G. Maxwell, 1818.

AMORY, Martha Babcock. *The Domestic and Artistic Life of John Singleton Copley*. Boston, 1882. Reprint, New York: Da Capo Press, 1969.

ARMITAGE, Shelly. *Kewpies and Beyond: The World of Rose O'Neill*. Jackson: University of Mississippi Press, 1994.

ARMSTRONG, Maitland. *Day Before Yesterday: Reminiscences of a Varied Life*. New York: Charles Scribner's Sons, 1920.

ASTOR, Gavin. *The Gardens at Hever Castle*. Norwich: Jarrold and Sons, 1982.

ATHERTON, Gertrude. *American Wives and English Husbands*. New York: Dodd, Mead, 1898.

BACON, Henry. *Parisian Art and Artists*. Boston: J. R. Osgood, 1883.

BAILEY, Eileen A., ed. *Crannog to Castle*. Edinburgh: James Burnett of Leys, 2000.

BALLARD, Phillada. "Rus in Urbe: Joseph Chamberlain's Gardens at Highbury, Moor Green, Birmingham, 1879–1914." *Garden History* 14 (Spring 1986): 61–84.

"Batemans, Sussex, the Residence of Mr. Rudyard Kipling," *Country Life* 24 (August 15, 1908): 224–33.

BECKER, Robert. *Nancy Lancaster*. New York: Alfred A. Knopf, 1996.

BEISWANGER, William L. "The Temple in the Garden: Thomas Jefferson's Vision of the Monticello Landscape." *Eighteenth Century Life* 8 (January 1983): 170–88.

BERENSON, Bernard. *Aesthetics and History in the Visual Arts*. New York: Pantheon, 1948.

———. *Sketch for a Self-Portrait*. London: Constable, 1949.

BRANDON, Ruth. *A Capitalist Romance: Singer and the Sewing Machine*. Philadelphia: J. B. Lippincott, 1977.

———. *The Dollar Princesses: Sagas of Upward Nobility 1870–1914*. New York: Alfred A. Knopf, 1980.

BRIZARDEL, Yvon. *American Painters in Paris*. New York: The Macmillan Company, 1969.

BROOKS, Van Wyck. *Dream of Arcadia: American Writers and Artists in Italy 1760–1915*. New York: E. P. Dutton, 1958.

BULLET, Emma. "MacMonnies the Sculptor Working Hard as a Painter." *Brooklyn Daily Eagle* (September 8, 1901).

BURROUGHS, Alan. *John Greenwood in America 1745–1752*. Andover, Massachusetts: Addison Gallery of American Art, 1943.

CABOT, Francis H. *The Greater Perfection: The Story of the Gardens at Les Quatres Vents* (New York: W. W. Norton/Hortus Press, 2001).

CAPPON, Lester J. *The Adams-Jefferson Letters*, Vol. I: *1777–1804*. Chapel Hill: The University of North Carolina Press, 1959.

CARLEY, Lionel. *Delius: A Life in Letters*. Cambridge: Harvard University Press, 1983.

CARLISLE, Carla. *South-Facing Slope*. Bury St. Edmunds: Snakeshead Press, 2001.

CARTWRIGHT, Julia Mary. *A Bright Remembrance 1851–1925*. London: Weidenfeld and Nicholson, 1989.

CARVALLO, Robert and Henri. *The Chateau de Villandry*. Paris: Editions Plume, 1998.

CERIO, Edwin. *The Masque of Capri*. London: Thomas Nelson and Sons, 1957.

CHANLER, Margaret Terry. *Autumn in the Valley*. Boston: Little, Brown, 1936.

———. *Roman Spring: Memoirs*. Boston: Little Brown, 1934.

CHERNOW, Ron. *The House of Morgan*. New York: Atlantic Monthly Press, 1990.

CHURCH, Alfred. *Pliny's Letters*. Philadelphia: J. B. Lippincott and Company, 1872.

CLARKE, Ethne. *Hidcote: The Making of a Garden*. London: Michael Joseph, 1989.

CLEWS, Maris. *Once Upon a Time at La Napoule*. Beverly, Massachusetts: Memoirs Unlimited, 1998.

CONWAY, John Joseph. *Footprints of Famous Americans in Paris*. London: John Lane, 1912.

CRANE, Sylvia E. *The White Silence: Greenough, Powers, and Crawford, American Sculptors in Nineteenth-Century Italy*. Coral Gables, Florida: University of Miami Press, 1972.

CRANE, Walter. *An Artist's Reminiscences*. London: Methuen and Company, 1907.

CUTLER, Phoebe. "Villas of Rome and Gardens at Home." *Journal of the New England Garden History Society* 8 (Fall 2000): 3–12.

DAVIS, Richard Harding. *About Paris*. New York: Harper and Brothers, 1895.

DE KAY, Charles. "A Villa in Capri." *Architectural Record* 12 (May 1902): 71–92.

DE MARE, Marie. *G. P. A. Healy: American Artist*. New York: David McKay, 1954.

DE NAVARRO, Mary Anderson. *A Few More Memories*. London: Hutchinson and Company, 1936.

DE POLIGNAC, Princesse Edmond. "Memoirs." *Horizon* 12 (August 1945): 110–41.

DE WOLFE, Elsie. *After All*. New York: Harper & Brothers, 1935.

Detroit, University of Michigan, Kelsey Museum of Archaeology. *In Pursuit of Antiquity: Thomas Spencer Jerome and the Bay of Naples*. 1983.

DICKEY, Page. *Breaking Ground*. New York: Workman, 1997.

DONNELLY, Honoria Murphy. *Sara and Gerald: Villa America and After*. New York: Times Books, 1982.

DUBOSE, Louise Jones. *Enigma: The Career of Blondelle Malone*. Columbia: University of South Carolina Press, 1963.

DULLES, Foster Rhea. *Americans Abroad: Two Centuries of European Travel*. Ann Arbor: University of Michigan Press, 1964.

DUNCAN, William Cary. *The Amazing Madame Jumel*. New York: Frederick A. Stokes Company, 1935.

DURYEA, Hendrick V. "The Intimate Garden of Miss Elsie de Wolfe at Villa Trianon at Versailles, France." *The Book of Gardens and Gardening*, edited by Reginald T. Townsend. Garden City, New York: Doubleday, Page & Company, 1924.

DWIGHT, Eleanor. *Edith Wharton: An Extraordinary Life*. New York: Harry N. Abrams, 1994.

————. "Edith Wharton's French Landscapes." *Architectural Digest* (March 1994) 84–90.

E.C. "A Riviera Garden: Sainte-Claire le Château, Hyères." *Country Life* (November 3, 1928): 610–13.

EDEL, Leon. *Life of Henry James*. Vols. III–V. Philadelphia: J. B. Lipppincott, 1962–72.

————, ed. *Henry James Letters*. Vols. I–IV. Cambridge: Harvard University Press, 1974–1984.

EDEN, F. *A Garden in Venice*. London: Country Life, 1903.

ELGOOD, George S., and Gertrude Jekyll. *Some English Gardens*. London: Longman, Green, 1905 (3rd edition).

ELLIOTT, Brent. *Victorian Gardens*. London: B.T. Batsford Ltd., 1986.

ELLIOTT, Maud Howe. *My Cousin F. Marion Crawford*. New York: The Macmillan Company, 1934.

————. *Roma Beata: Letters from the Eternal City*. Boston: Little, Brown, 1904.

FAIRWEATHER, Catherine. *La Dolce Vita: Living in Italy*. New York: Little, Brown, 2001.

FLANDERS, Judith. *A Circle of Sisters*. London: Penguin Books, 2002.

FLEXNER, James Thomas. *Gilbert Stuart*. New York: Alfred A. Knopf, 1955.

FORMAN, H. Buxton. "An American Studio in Florence." *The Manhattan* 3 (June 1884): 527–39.

FOSTER, Kathleen A., and Michael Quick. *Edwin Austin Abbey, 1852–1911*. New Haven: Yale University Art Gallery, 1973.

"Frederick MacMonnies' Home Near Paris." *Town and Country* (February 3, 1906): 16.

Frederick William MacMonnies (1863–1937), Mary Fairchild MacMonnies (1888–1946). Vernon, France: Musée Municipal A.G. Poulain, 1988.

FROTHINGHAM, Eugenia Brooks. *Youth and I*. Boston: Houghton Mifflin, 1938.

GARVIN. J. L. *The Life of Joseph Chamberlain*. London: Macmillan & Company, 1933.

GAY, Walter. *Memoirs*. New York: Harry N. Abrams, 1930.

GERDTS, William H. "The American Artist at Grez." *The Painters in Grez-sur-Loing*. Tokyo: Japanese Association of Museum, 2000.

————. "The Arch-Apostle of the Dab-and-Spot School: John Singer Sargent As an Impressionist." *John Singer Sargent*. New York: Whitney Museum of American Art, 1986.

————. *Monet's Giverny: An Impressionist Colony*. New York: Abbeville Press, 1993.

GILL, Anton. *Peggy Guggenheim: The Life of an Art Addict*. London: HarperCollins, 2001.

GOLDSMITH, Barbara. *Other Powers*. New York: HarperCollins, 1998.

GOROKHOFF, Galina. *Love Locked Out: The Memoirs of Anna Lea Merritt*. Boston: Museum of Fine Arts, 1982.

GREATOREX, Eleanor. "Mary Fairchild MacMonnies." *Godey's Magazine* (May 1893): 624–632.

GUGGENHEIM, Peggy. *Confessions of an Art Addict*. 1960. Reprint Hopewell, N.J.: Ecco Press, 1979.

HADLEY, Rollin Van N., ed. *Letters of Bernard Berenson and Isabella Stewart Gardner*. Boston: Northeastern University Press, 1987.

HALBERSTAM, Davis. "A Wonderful Life." *Town and Country* (December 2000): 296–98.

HALE, Susan, ed. *Life and Letters of Thomas Gold Appleton*. New York: D. Appleton and Company, 1885.

HAWTHORNE, Nathaniel. *The Marble Faun*. 1859. Reprint New York: New American Library, 1961.

HILL, May Brawley. *Grandmother's Garden: The Old-Fashioned American Garden 1865–1915*. New York: Harry N. Abrams, 1995.

HILLARD, George Stillmann. *Six Months in Italy*. Boston: 1847.

HITCHMOUGH, Wendy. *Arts and Crafts Gardens*. New York: Rizzoli, 1998.

HOBHOUSE, Penelope. "The Gardens of the Villa La Foce." *Hortus* l, no. 3 (1987): 73–81.

HONOUR, Hugh, and John Fleming. *The Venetian Hours of Henry James, Whistler and Sargent*. Boston: Little, Brown, 1991.

HOOPER, Lucy. *Under the Tricolor*. Philadelphia: J. B. Lippincott, 1880.

HOWELLS, William Dean. *Venetian Life*. New York: Heard and Houghton, 1866.

HOYT, Edwin P., Jr. *The House of Morgan*. New York: Dodd, Mead and Company, 1966.

HUDSON, Gertrude Reese, ed. *Browning to His American Friends (1841–1890)*. New York: Barnes and Noble, 1965.

HUMPHREYS, Mary Gay. *Catherine Schuyler*. New York: Charles Scribner's Sons, 1897.

HUNT, Leigh. *The Autobiography of Leigh Hunt*. New York: Dutton, 1903.

HYDE, H. Montgomery. *Henry James at Home*. New York: Farrar, Straus and Giroux, 1969.

IRVING, Washington. *The Sketchbook of Geoffrey Crayon*. 1819. Reprint, New York: A. L. Burt, 1860.

JACKSON-STOPS, Gervase. *An English Arcadia, 1600–1900*. London: National Trust, 1992.

JAMES, Henry. *Italian Hours*. 1909. Reprint New York: Penguin, 1992.

_____. *Roderick Husdon*. 1875. Reprint London: Penguin, 1986.

_____. *William Wetmore Story and His Friends*. 1906. Reprint New York: DaCapo Press, 1969.

JEKYLL, Gertrude, and Lawrence Weaver. *Arts and Crafts Gardens*. 1912. Reprint London: Antiques Collectors Club, 1997.

JOASS, J. J. "On Gardening with Descriptions of Some Formal Gardens in Scotland." *The Studio* (1897).

JOHNSTON, Johanna. *Mrs. Satan: The Incredible Saga of Victoria Woodhull*. London: MacMillan, 1967.

JONES, Louisa. *Gardens in Provence*. Paris: Flammarion, 1992.

KAPLAN, Fred, ed. *Traveling in Italy with Henry James*. New York: William Morrow, 1994.

KAVALER, Lucy. *The Astors*. New York: Dodd, Mead, 1966.

KENIN, Richard. *Return to Albion: Americans in England, 1760–1940*. Washington, D.C.: National Portrait Gallery, Smithsonian Institution, 1979.

KILMER, Nicholas. *Frederick Carl Frieseke*. Princeton: Princeton University Press, 2001.

_____. *A Place in Normandy*. New York: Henry Holt, 1997.

KIMBOROUGH, Sara Dodge. *Drawn from Life*. Jackson: University Press of Mississippi, 1976.

LAMONTAGNE, Michele and Jean-Claude. "Rudkin's Rooms." *Horticulture* 71 (October 1993): 42–47.

LATHROP, Henrietta S. "The Real Broadway." *The Outlook* 53 (May 30, 1896): 996.

LE CLAIR, Robert Charles. *Three American Travelers in England: James Russell Lowell, Henry Adams, Henry James*. Westport, Conn.: Greenwood Press, 1978.

LEES-MILNE, Alvide. "Ninfa: A Garden in the Ruins of a Town." *Hortus* 2 (Spring 1998): 40–49.

LEITH, Royal W. "The Expatriate Years of Henry Roderick Newman." *Antiques* (April 1996): 574–83.

Letters and Papers of John Singleton Copley and Henry Pelham 1739–1776. Boston: Massachusetts Historical Society, 1914.

LEVENSTEIN, Harvey. *Seductive Journeys: American Tourists in France from Jefferson to the Jazz Age*. Chicago: University of Chicago Press, 1998.

LEWIS, Alfred Allan. *Ladies and Not-so-gentle Women*. New York: Viking, 2000.

LEWIS, R. W. B. *Edith Wharton*. New York: Harper and Row, 1975.

LOOMIS, Susan Hermann. *On Rue Tatin*. New York: Broadway Books, 2001.

LOPEZ, Claude-Anne. *Mon Cher Papa: Franklin and the Ladies of Paris*. New Haven: Yale University Press, 1966.

LORD, James. *A Gift for Admiration*. New York: Farrar, Straus and Giroux, 1997.

LOW, Will H. "In an Old French Garden." *Scribner's Magazine* (July 1902): 3-19.

LUBBOCK, Percy. *Portrait of Edith Wharton*. New York: Appleton Century Crofts, 1947.

LUHAN, Mabel Dodge. *European Experiences*. New York: Harcourt, Brace and Company, 1935.

"The Lure of the Golden Bowl." *Apollo* 118 (August 1983): 119–21.

MACCHESNEY, "Frederick Carl Frieseke." *Arts and Decoration* 3 (November 1912): 13–15.

_____. Clara. "Frieseke Tells Some of the Secrets of His Art." *New York Times* (June 7, 1914): VI, 7.

MACCUBBIN, R. P., and Peter Martin, eds. *British and American Gardens in the Eighteenth Century*. Williamsburg: Colonial Williamsburg, 1984.

MACKENSIE, Faith Compton. *As Much as I Dare*. London: Collins, 1938.

MACNUTT, Francis Augustus. *A Papal Chamberlain*. London: Longmans, Green, 1936.

MARSH, Peter T. *Joseph Chamberlain: Entrepreneur in Politics*. New Haven: Yale University Press, 1994.

MCCANSE, Ralph Alan. *Titans and Kewpies: The Life and Art of Rose O'Neill*. New York: Vantage Press, 1968.

MCCULLOUGH, David. *John Adams*. New York: Simon and Schuster, 2001.

MCGOWAN ASSOCIATES. *Crathes Castle Historical Lansacape Survey*. Edinburgh: The National Trust for Scotland, 1997.

MCILHENNY, Henry P. "Glenveagh Castle, County Donegal." In Sybill Connolly and Helen Dillon. *In an Irish Garden*. London: Weidenfeld and Nicolson, 1986: 100–103.

MCLEAN, Elizabeth. "Town and Country Gardens in Eighteenth Century Philadelphia." *Eighteenth Century Life* 8 (January 1983) : 136–47.

MARTINDALE, Meredith. "Benjamin Franklin's Residence in Paris." *Antiques* 123 (August 1977): 262-73.

MARTINEAU, Mrs. Philip. *Gardening in Sunny Lands*. New York: Appleton, 1924.

MASSON, Georgina. *Italian Gardens*. New York: Harry N. Abrams, 1961.

_____. *Italian Villas and Palaces*. New York: Harry N. Abrams, 1959.

MATHEWS, Nancy Mowell. *Cassatt and Her Circle, Selected Letters*. New York: Abbeville Press, 1984.

MEREDITH, Michael, ed. *More Than Friend: The Letters of Robert Browning to Katharine de Kay Bronson*. Waco, Texas: Baylor University Press, 1985

MERRITT, Anna Lea. *An Artist's Garden*. London: George Allen and Sons, 1908.

_____. *A Hamlet in Old Hampshire*. London: Kegan Paul, 1902.

_____. "A Letter to Artists." *Lippincott's Monthly* 65 (March 1900): 463–69.

Metropolitan Museum of Art, New York. *Monet's Years at Giverny: Beyond Impressionism*. 1978.

MILLET, Frank D. "Home of the Indolent: The Island of Capri." *The Century Illustrated Monthly Magazine* 56 (October 1898): 853-858.

MOOREHEAD, Caroline. *Iris Origo: Marchesa of Val d'Orcia*. Boston: David R. Godine, 2000.

MORRIS, Gouverneur. *A Diary of the French Revolution*. New York: Charles Scribner's Sons, 1888.

MOWL, Timothy. *Gentlemen and Players: Gardeners of the English Landscape Garden*. Stroud, England: Sutton Publishing, 2000.

NEUBAUER, Erika. "The Garden Architecture of Cecil Pinsent." *Journal of Garden History* 3, no. 1 (1983): 35–48.

NORTON, Charles Eliot. *Notes of Travel and Study in Italy*. Boston: Houghton Mifflin, 1881.

O'KEEFE, Ciaran. *The History of Glenveagh*. Dublin: Office of Public Works, 1991.

OLSON, Stanley, Warren Adelson, and Richard Ormond. *Sargent at Broadway: The Impressionist Years*. New York: Universe Books, 1986.

ORIGO, Iris. *Images and Shadows*. New York: Harcourt, Brace, Jovanovich, 1970.

ORMOND, Richard, ed. *John Singer Sargent*. London: Tate Gallery, 1998.

OSBORNE, Carol M. "Lizzie Boott at Bellosguardo." In Irma B. Jaffe, ed. *The Italian Presence in American Art 1860–1920*. New York: Fordham University Press, 1992: 188–99.

OTTENWILL, David. *The Edwardian Garden*. New Haven: Yale University Press, 1989.

OWEN, Jane. "Twists and Turns." *The Garden* (May 1998): 344–51.

PARKER, Wyman W. *Henry Stevens of Vermont: An American Bookdealer in London 1845–1886*. Amsterdam: N. Israel, 1963.

PAVORD, Anna. *Hidcote Manor Garden*. London: The National Trust, 1993.

PEALE, Rembrandt. *Notes on Italy written during a tour in 1829 to 1830*. Philadelphia: Carey and Lea, 1831.

PEARSON, Hesketh. *The Marrying Americans*. New York: Coward, McCann, 1961.

PENNELL, Elizabeth Robbins. *Nights: Rome–Venice in the Aesthetic Eighties, London–Paris in the Fighting Nineties*. Philadelphia: J. B. Lippincott Company, 1916.

PERRY, Lilla Cabot. "Reminiscences of Claude Monet from 1889 to 1909." *American Magazine of Art* 28 (March 1927): 119–25.

PHILLIPS, Mary E. *Reminiscences of William Wetmore Story*. Chicago and New York: Rand, McNally and Company, 1897.

PISANO, Ronald G. *A Leading Spirit in American Art*. Seattle: Henry Art Gallery, 1983.

PLOWDEN, Helen Haseltine. *William Stanley Haseltine*. London: Frederick Muller, 1947.

PRATT, Charles A. *Italian Gardens*. 1894. Reprint Portland, Ore.: Sagapress, 2000.

QUEST-RITSON, Charles. *The English Garden Abroad*. London: Viking, 1992.

QUICK, Michael. *American Expatriate Painters of the Late Nineteenth Century*. Dayton, Ohio: Dayton Art Museum, 1967.

RANDALL, Lillian M.C., ed. *Diary of George A. Lucas*. Princeton: Princeton University Press, 1979.

RATHER, Susan. "Rome and the American Academy." In Irma B. Jaffe, ed. *The Italian Presence in American Art 1860–1920*. New York: Fordham University Press, 1992: 214–228.

RICE, Howard C., Jr. *L'Hôtel de Langéac: Thomas Jefferson's Paris Residence*. Monticello: Thomas Jefferson Foundation, 1947.

———. *Thomas Jefferson's Paris*. Princeton: Princeton University Press, 1976.

RICHARDS, Laura E., and Maude Howe Elliott. *Julia Ward Howe*. 2 vols. New York: Houghton Mifflin Company, 1916.

RIEDER, William. *A Charmed Couple: The Art and Life of Walter and Matilda Gay*. New York: Harry N. Abrams, 2000.

"The Right Hon. J. Chamberlain—His Home and Garden." *Journal of Horticulture* 32 (March 12, 1896): 227–233.

ROBINSON, Joyce Henri, and Derrick C. Cartwright. *An Interlude in Giverny*. University Park: Palmer Museum of Art, Pennsylvania State University, 2001.

RODRIGUEZ, Suzanne. *Wild Heart*. New York: HarperCollins, 2002.

ROGERS, George C., Jr. "Gardens and Landscapes in Eighteenth Century South Carolina." *Eighteenth Century Life* 8 (January 1983): 148–58.

ROSS, Ishbel. *The Expatriates*. New York: Thomas Y. Crowell Company, 1970.

RUSTICUS, "A Letter to Pliny the Younger Relating to the Villa Castello on Capri," *House and Garden* 2 (August 1902): 343–354.

SACKVILLE-WEST, Vita. "Hidcote Manor." *Journal of the Royal Horticultural Society* 64 (November 1949): 476–81.

SAMUELS, Ernest. *Bernard Berenson: The Making of a Legend*. Cambridge: Harvard University Press, 1987.

SANDERSON, John. *The American in Paris*. Philadelphia: Carey and Hart, 1839.

SAWITZKY, William. *Matthew Pratt: 1734–1803*. New York: New York Historical Society, 1942.

SCHOENBRUN, David. *Triumphs in Paris: The Exploits of Benjamin Franklin*. New York: Harper and Row, 1976.

SECREST, Meryle. *Being Bernard Berenson*. New York: Holt, Rinehart and Winston, 1979.

———. *Between Me and Life: A Biography of Romaine Brooks*. New York: Doubleday & Company, 1974.

SELLIN, David. *Americans in Brittany and Normandy, 1860–1915*. Phoenix, Arizona: Phoenix Art Museum, 1982.

SHAND-TUCCI, Douglass. *The Art of Scandal: The Life and Times of Isabella Stewart Gardner*. New York: Harper, Collins, 1998.

SHACKELFORD, George Green. *Thomas Jefferson's Travels in Europe 1784–1789*. Baltimore: Johns Hopkins University Press, 1995.

SHEPPERSON, Archibald B. *John Paradise and Lucy Ludwell*. Richmond: Deitz Press, 1942.

SHERWOOD, Dolly. *Harriet Hosmer American Sculptor 1830–1908*. Columbia: University of Missouri Press, 1991.

SIMPSON, Marc. "Windows on the Past: Edwin Austin Abbey and Francis Davis Millet in England." *The American Art Journal* 12, no. 3 (1990): 64–89.

SKELMERSDALE, Lord. "The Gardens at Ninfa, Italy," *Journal of the Royal Horticultural Society* 94 (June 1969): 246–52.

SMEDLEY, Constance. "The Expatriates III: The American Colony in London." *Bookman* 25 (July-August 1907): 484–95.

SMITH, Jane S. *Elsie de Wolfe, a Life in the High Style*. New York: Atheneum, 1982.

SORIA, Regina. *Elihu Vedder: American Visionary Artist in Rome*. Rutherford, N.J.: Fairleigh Dickinson University Press, 1970.

SPINK, Nesta R. *James McNeill Whistler Lithographs from the Collection of Steven Block*. Washington, D.C.: Trust for Museum Exhibitions, 2000.

STOWE, William W. *Going Abroad: European Travel in Nineteenth-Century American Culture*. Princeton: Princeton University Press, 1994.

STRACHEY, Barbara, and Jayne Samuels, eds. *Mary Berenson: A Self-Portrait from Her Diaries and Letters*. New York: W.W. Norton, 1983.

SWIGGETT, Howard. *The Extraordinary Mr. Morris*. Garden City, New York: Doubleday and Company, 1952.

T. "The Villa Sylvia, the Property of Mr. Ralph Curtis." *Country Life* (July 16, 1910): 90–97.

TAYLOR, G. C. "The Borders at Floors Castle," *Country Life* 68 (December 6, 1930): 761–64.

Titled Americans. New York: Street and Smith, 1890.

TINTNER, Adeline. *The Cosmopolitan World of Henry James*. Baton Rouge: Louisiana State University Press, 1991.

TOMKINS, Calvin. *Living Well Is the Best Revenge*. New York: Viking Press, 1962. Reprint New York: Signet, 1971.

TRAFTON, Adeline. *An American Girl Abroad*. Boston: Lee and Shepard, 1892.

TREVES, G. Arthur. *The Golden Ring: The Anglo-Florentines 1847–1862*. London: 1956.

Tribute of Boston Merchants to the Memory of Joshua Bates. Boston: John Wilson and Son, 1864.

TROLLOP, Thomas Adolphus. *What I Remember*. New York: Harper & Brothers, 1890.

TUCKERMAN, Henry. *A Memorial to Horatio Greenough*. New York: G. P. Putnam, 1853.

TURNER, A. Richard. *La Pietra, Florence: A Family and a Villa*. Florence: Olivares, 2002.

VANCE, William. *America's Rome*. New Haven: Yale University Press, 1989.

VEDDER, Elihu. *The Digressions of V*. New York: Houghton Mifflin, 1910.

VENISON, Tony. "From Rectory to Roses," *Country Life* 182, no. 24 (June 16, 1988): 150–55.

WADDINGTON, Mary King. *Italian Letters of a Diplomat's Wife*. New York: Charles Scribner's Sons, 1905.

WARSHAWSKY, Abel. *The Memories of an American Impressionist*. Kent, Ohio: Kent State University Press, 1980.

WATSON, Winslow, ed. *Men and Times of the Revolution, or Memoirs of Elkanah Watson (1777–1842)*. New York: Dana and Company, 1856.

WEAVER, William. "A Legendary Italian Garden," *New York Times*, Travel Section (March 30, 1997): 13–14.

WEINBERG, H. Barbara. "The Career of Francis Davis Millet." *Archives of American Art Journal* 17, no. 1 (1977): 2–18.

_____. *The Lure of Paris: Nineteenth-Century American Painters and Their French Teachers*. New York: Abbeville Press, 1991.

WEINTRAUB, Stanley. *The London Yankees: Portraits of American Writers and Artists in England, 1894–1914*. New York: Harcourt, Brace, Jovanovich, 1981.

WELLS, Patricia. *At Home in Provence*. London: Kyle Cathe Ltd., 1998.

WHARTON, Edith. *A Backward Glance* (1933). New York: Simon and Schuster, 1998.

_____. *French Ways and Their Meaning* (1919). Lee, Mass.: Berkshire House Publishers, 1997.

WHITING, Lilian. *Italy the Magic Land*. Boston: Little, Brown and Company, 1910.

WHITLOCK, Stephen. "An American Grows in France." *Garden Design* 18 (October 1999): 66–73.

WIEBENSON, Dora. *The Picturesque Garden in France*. Princeton: Princeton University Press, 1978.

WILKES, George. *Americans in Paris*. Garden City, New York: Doubleday and Company, 1969.

WOODRESS, James L. *Howells and Italy*. Durham, North Carolina: Duke University Press, 1952.

WRIGHT, Nathalia. *American Novelists in Italy. The Discoverers: Allston to James*. Philadelphia: University of Pennsylvania Press, 1965.

ZWERDLING, Alex. *Improvised Europeans: American Literary Expatriates and the Siege of London*. New York: Basic Books, 1998.

Index